S0-CCJ-877

Healthy Living
Made Easy

We created this cookbook—our first—just for you. These are the dishes that nourish us and inspire us ... the ones we cook again and again. The best part? Every delicious recipe can be cooked in 30 minutes or less using simple, wholesome ingredients, almost all of which you can find at member-only prices right on Thrive Market.

At Thrive Market, our mission is simple: make healthy living easy and affordable for everyone. Think of this cookbook as an extension of that vision. It's tangible proof you don't have to spend a lot of time or money to cook a delicious meal for your family that's also mindful of your diet and values.

The recipes in this book are also a reflection of our community. Some come from our team, but many were shared with us by members like you and others contributed by our longtime friends and partners, thought leaders like Amanda Chantal Bacon (Moon Juice), Mark Sisson (Primal Kitchen), and Melissa Urban (Whole30©).

A heartfelt thank-you to each of them—and to you, too. Thank you for taking your health and that of our planet into your own hands, for choosing to be part of our community, and for supporting Thrive Market's mission to make healthy living accessible to all.

I hope these healthy recipes quickly become as beloved in your home as they have been in ours.

Happy cooking!

–Nick Green, Thrive Market Co-Founder & CEO

We dedicate this cookbook to
our incredible member community.

Thank you for supporting our mission of
making healthy living accessible to all.

We wouldn't be here without you.

Table of Contents

Gluten-free? Have a nut allergy?
Use these icons to find recipes that fit your lifestyle.

Visit **ThriveMarket.com** to explore 90+ values and shop the healthy products that work for you.

Gluten-Free

Grain-Free

Dairy-Free

Vegan

Egg-Free

Nut-Free

Our Partners in Healthy Living

 Amanda Chantal Bacon (@amandachantalbacon) is the Founder of Moon Juice, a wellness brand rooted in adaptogens and the wisdom of alternative medicine. Over 10 years, the brand's supplements and clean beauty products have attracted a cult following.

 Thomas & Amber DeLauer (@thomasdelauer & @amberdelauer) are authors and keto influencers who reside in the central coast of California. Thomas runs a nutrition and business-performance coaching business; Amber is a blogger and mom.

 Rachael DeVaux (@rachaelsgoodeats) is a registered dietitian, personal trainer, and food blogger with a passion for travel. She is based in Seattle.

 Dr. Mark Hyman (@drmarkhyman) is a physician and advocate for using food as medicine. A 14-time *New York Times* bestselling author, he focuses on cooking with real food and regenerative farming.

 Dr. Mikhail Varshavski D.O. (@doctor.mike), also known as Doctor Mike, is a board-certified family medicine physician, media personality, educator, and dog dad. Through his TV appearances and successful YouTube channel, he combats misinformation and promotes balanced nutrition.

 Chris Kresser (@chriskresser) is a functional medicine clinician, an educator, and the bestselling author of *The Paleo Cure*. Having overcome chronic illness with ancestral nutrition, he now helps others optimize their health by eating right.

 Megan Mitchell (@chefmeganmitch) is an LA-based chef and food stylist focusing on healthy, approachable, and delicious cooking. She's also the host of Thrive Market's *Prep School* series.

 Jeannette Ogden (@shutthekaleup) is the influencer behind shutthekaleup, a food and lifestyle blog. A proud California native, she advocates for balanced, real-food eating and body positivity.

 Bobby Parrish (@flavcity) is the host of the popular YouTube channel and blog FlavCity. His daily recipes include lots of keto-friendly and gluten-free options.

Pamela Salzman (@pamelasalzman) is a SoCal-based cooking instructor and cookbook author. Her recipes feature comfort foods made from minimally processed ingredients and meals that come together in minutes.

Caitlin Shoemaker (@frommybowl) is a Washington-based yoga instructor and the blogger behind From My Bowl. She creates plant-based recipes with easy-to-find, affordable ingredients that pack a flavorful punch.

Wes Shoemaker (@highfalutinlowcarb) is the host behind the YouTube series Highfalutin' Low Carb, where he tests different keto-friendly recipes on the internet to find the best ones. Based in San Diego, he is also a proud dog dad.

Mark Sisson (@marksdailyapple) is the paleo expert, former endurance athlete, and founder of the Primal Blueprint lifestyle behind the popular paleo blog Mark's Daily Apple. He also founded Primal Kitchen, a line of real-food condiments, sauces, dressings, and more.

Shawn Stevenson (@shawnmodel) is a nutritionist and author of the *USA TODAY* bestselling book *Eat Smarter*. After being diagnosed with a spinal condition at age 20, he embraced the power of food to transform his mind and body.

Melissa Urban (@melissau) is a bestselling author and the Co-Founder and CEO of Whole30®. In 2009, she began a 30-day self-experiment based on real-food eating, and has since touted its energy-boosting, sleep-improving, craving-busting benefits.

JJ Virgin (@jj.virgin) is a *New York Times* bestselling author, a triple board-certified health expert, and a mom of two. She's helped over a million people look and feel their best by eating and exercising smarter.

Danielle Walker (@daniellewalker) is a *New York Times* bestselling cookbook author (*Against All Grain, Meals Made Simple, Celebrations*, and *Eat What You Love*), health advocate, wellness expert, and self-trained chef.

Katie Wells (@wellnessmama) is the founder of Wellness Mama, a blog and podcast focused on parenting and healthy living. She shares natural health remedies and recipes for meals with simple, minimally processed ingredients.

Robb Wolf (@dasrobbwolf) is a bestselling author and former research biochemist. On a mission to help others fight inflammation, he shares tips on paleo, keto, and gluten-free eating.

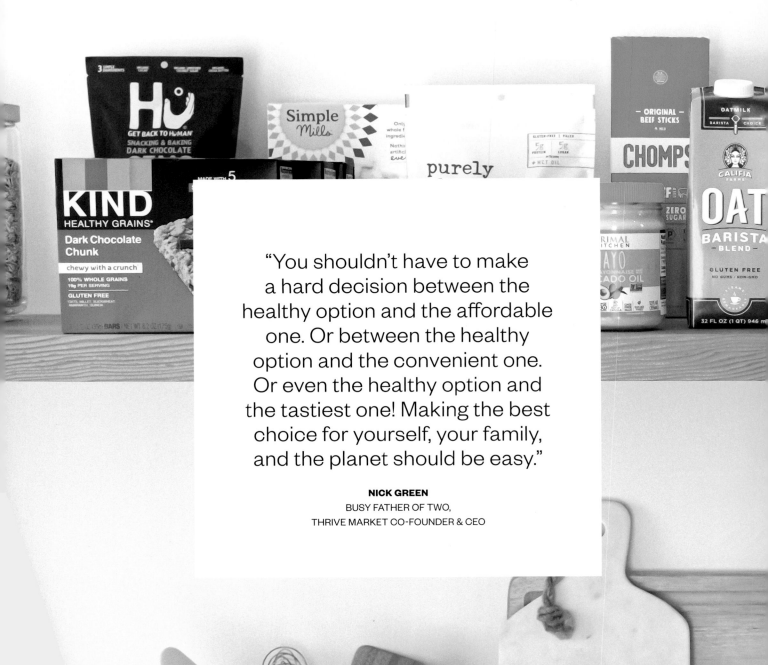

"You shouldn't have to make a hard decision between the healthy option and the affordable one. Or between the healthy option and the convenient one. Or even the healthy option and the tastiest one! Making the best choice for yourself, your family, and the planet should be easy."

NICK GREEN
BUSY FATHER OF TWO,
THRIVE MARKET CO-FOUNDER & CEO

Thrive Market was born and bred in Los Angeles, a city known for healthy living. We want to make it possible for everyone to live their healthiest, happiest life—and to help build a better world in the process, with the highest-quality organic and sustainable products.

From our home to yours, we're so grateful to be able to help you save time, save money, and live your healthiest life.

Breakfast

Good old-fashioned rolled oats are one of the most versatile pantry staples, whether in a hot bowl of morning oatmeal, whizzed in the food processor until they become oat flour, or blended into a smoothie. Now, meet your new favorite way to eat them: these chewy, fruity granola jam bars.

BREAKFAST

Granola Jam Bars

Dairy-Free   Vegan   Egg-Free

INGREDIENTS

Cooking Spray

1 3/4 cups Thrive Market Organic All-Purpose Flour

1 3/4 cups Thrive Market Organic Gluten-Free Rolled Oats

1 cup Thrive Market Organic Walnuts, coarsely chopped

1 cup Thrive Market Organic Coconut Sugar

1/2 teaspoon Thrive Market Organic Ground Nutmeg

1/2 teaspoon kosher salt

1 teaspoon Thrive Market Baking Soda

3/4 cup melted Thrive Market Organic Virgin Coconut Oil

1 1/4 cups Thrive Market Organic Fruit Spread (any flavor you like)

INSTRUCTIONS

Preheat oven to 350°F. Spray a 9-inch by 13-inch baking dish with cooking spray. Line the bottom with parchment paper. Spray the parchment paper with cooking spray and set aside.

Whisk flour, oats, walnuts, sugar, nutmeg, salt, and baking soda in a large bowl. Pour in the oil and stir until mixture is coated with all the oil.

Press 3/4 cup of the oat mixture onto the bottom of the baking dish. Spread an even layer of jam on the oat mixture. Sprinkle the remaining crust on top. Bake for 25 to 30 minutes, until the crust is golden brown.

Let cool completely before cutting. Store in an airtight container in the refrigerator for up to 2 weeks.

Scan here to shop the recipe

If you've got a few eggs, some tasty toppings, and a single pan, you've got brunch. Give your br⌐__ lively southwestern kick from savory chorizo, creamy avocado, and tangy salsa. This simple scramble is courtesy of **Shawn Stevenson**, author and host of The Model Health Show.

BREAKFAST

Southwest Chorizo Scramble

Gluten-Free   Grain-Free   Dairy-Free   Nut-Free

INGREDIENTS

1/4 pound ground chorizo

4 large eggs, whisked

1/4 teaspoon Thrive Market Organic Turmeric Powder

Sea salt and black pepper, to taste

1/4 cup Thrive Market Organic Salsa

1 large avocado, peeled, pitted, and sliced

INSTRUCTIONS

Heat a sauté pan over medium heat. Add the chorizo and cook until lightly browned, about 5 minutes.

Add the eggs and turmeric and season lightly with salt and pepper. Scramble the eggs, stirring with a spatula, for about 3 minutes.

Transfer the scramble to plates and top with salsa and avocado slices.

Scan here to shop the recipe

Here's a breakfast that will please kids and adults alike. A combination of nuts, seeds, dried fruit, and maple syrup makes these cookies both crunchy and chewy—while packing a nutritional punch that'll last until lunch. Plus, they're just plain fun to eat.

BREAKFAST

Superfood Breakfast Cookies

Gluten-Free　Grain-Free　Dairy-Free　Vegan　Egg-Free

INGREDIENTS

1/4 cup Thrive Market Organic Pumpkin Seeds

1/2 cup Thrive Market Organic Walnuts

1/2 cup Thrive Market Organic Raw Cashews

1/4 cup Thrive Market Organic Shredded Coconut, unsweetened

1 cup Thrive Market Organic Coconut Chips

1/2 teaspoon Thrive Market Organic Ground Ginger

1 tablespoon Thrive Market Organic Ground Flaxseed

1/2 teaspoon salt

3/4 cup Thrive Market Organic Raw Almonds, coarsely chopped

3/4 cup mixed dried berries (try Thrive Market Organic Goji Berries, Organic Mulberries, and Organic Seedless Raisins)

3 ripe bananas, mashed

1/4 cup Thrive Market Organic Virgin Coconut Oil, melted

1 tablespoon Thrive Market Organic Maple Syrup

1 teaspoon Thrive Market Organic Vanilla Extract

INSTRUCTIONS

Preheat oven to 350°F and line a baking sheet with parchment paper. In a blender or food processor, coarsely grind together pumpkin seeds, walnuts, cashews, and shredded coconut.

Pour mixture into a large bowl and mix with coconut chips, ground ginger, ground flaxseed, salt, almonds, and mixed dried berries.

In a small bowl, whisk together the mashed bananas, coconut oil, maple syrup, and vanilla extract. Pour wet ingredients into nut and seed mixture and mix to thoroughly combine.

With a 1 1/2-inch to 2-inch scoop, scoop out batter and place 1 inch apart on baking sheet. Bake for 10 to 15 minutes, rotating the sheet halfway through the baking time.

When cookies are golden brown, remove from oven and let cool before serving.

Scan here to shop the recipe

A classic diner stack made extra wholesome—that's what this recipe promises. New to quinoa flo
a similar look and feel to all-purpose wheat flour, but is naturally gluten-free, and provides both protein and
fiber. In this recipe, quinoa flour transforms your go-to morning feast into something unique.

BREAKFAST

Quinoa Pancakes

Gluten-Free   Dairy-Free

INGREDIENTS

1/2 cup Thrive Market Organic Quinoa Flour

2 teaspoons Thrive Market Baking Powder

1/2 teaspoon Thrive Market Organic Ground Cinnamon

1/4 teaspoon Thrive Market Organic Ground Nutmeg

1/2 teaspoon sea salt

1 egg

1/4 cup water

2 tablespoons Thrive Market Organic Apple Sauce

2 tablespoons Thrive Market Organic Maple Syrup, plus more for serving

Thrive Market Organic Virgin Coconut Oil, for cooking

1 cup blueberries

INSTRUCTIONS

In a large bowl, whisk quinoa flour, baking powder, cinnamon, nutmeg, and salt.

In a small bowl, whisk egg, water, apple sauce, and maple syrup.
Fold wet ingredients into dry and stir until just combined. Let the batter sit for 3 to 5 minutes, until it expands slightly.

In a nonstick skillet, melt coconut oil (enough to coat the pan) over medium heat. When the oil is shimmering, add a 1/4-cup scoop of batter and use the bottom of the measuring cup to flatten it. Cook until golden, about 3 to 4 minutes. Flip and cook for another 1 to 2 minutes. Repeat with remaining batter.

In the same skillet, add blueberries and let them blister, about 2 minutes. Serve pancakes stacked on a plate with blueberries spooned on top, plus extra maple syrup as desired.

Scan here to shop the recipe

Yes, this smoothie recipe, from author and nutrition expert **Chris Kresser**, contains egg yolk—but don't be alarmed. It imparts supremely creamy texture along with protein and vitamins. Rich coconut milk, juicy blueberries, and buttery macadamia nuts (either soaked in water overnight or in boiling water for 10–20 minutes right before using) are the flavors that really sing.

BREAKFAST

Blueberry & Macadamia Smoothie

Gluten-Free   Grain-Free   Dairy-Free

INGREDIENTS

1 cup blueberries,
fresh or frozen

1/2 cup Thrive Market Organic
Raw Macadamia Nuts, soaked

1 cup Thrive Market Organic
Almond Beverage

1/2 cup Thrive Market
Organic Coconut Milk

1 egg yolk

INSTRUCTIONS

Place all of the ingredients in a high-speed blender and blend until smooth. If the smoothie is thicker than desired, add an additional splash of almond or coconut milk.

*Scan here to
shop the recipe*

Coffee Grown for Good

Thrive Market sourcing guru (and Chief Merchandising Officer) Jeremiah McElwee tells us about the Peruvian families that grow and harvest Thrive Market Organic Coffee Beans.

Tell us about this special coffee program in Peru. We buy all of our beans directly from a small-scale coffee farming cooperative that grows its beans using sustainable, regenerative agriculture techniques. For example, they grow the coffee plants on the side of a mountain interspersed with all kinds of fruit plants (this is known as intercropping). Additionally, the co-op recaptures its own water to use for farming and uses compost to improve soil quality. The group's regenerative efforts help to pull carbon out of the atmosphere and into the soil, which helps to reverse the effects of climate change.

The farmers, who are second- and third-generation coffee growers, were worried that their children would leave the farming community to seek a better life in big cities like Lima. They didn't believe that there were enough people out there who cared about regenerative agriculture and were willing to pay fair trade prices. When I told them how much our members care about sustainably and ethically sourced products, they were thrilled to be able to work with us. I think it's amazing that our members get to truly make a big difference for this community every time they enjoy Thrive Market Coffee.

So there's no middle man? Correct. Typically, big industry players will buy large amounts of coffee beans on the open market. But they won't know exactly where the beans are coming from or how they're grown. They may have a vague idea of the region where the coffee was sourced, but it's typically not from a fair trade cooperative where the crops are organic and regeneratively grown. In such a transaction, there's no transparency and minimal traceability, and there's no way of knowing whether the workers and farmers were paid fairly.

The difference with our coffee is that it's all coming from one source. That way we're able to spend time with the growers in their community. We can see that the quality of the beans is closely monitored. The farmers in the cooperative are experts at growing coffee and they have an amazing facility where they test every single batch for quality and consistency. They reject certain batches if they don't meet the quality standards required to be shipped to America. Our beans go through the same rigorous process at our master roaster, which is also a high-quality, accredited facility.

How does Thrive Market support the local community in Peru? Whenever you get involved in single-origin partnerships and you're moving from fair trade to direct trade—meaning you're agreeing to a price based on a fair market value for that region plus a premium so there's a living wage being provided—you're making a huge impact on your partners' lives. We wanted to find a way to partner with the Peruvian coffee co-op that wasn't just transactional and made them feel like they're part of the Thrive Market family.

Our Thrive Gives Mission Leader and I traveled to Peru as a team so we could spend time in the community and better understand their needs. We didn't want to guess what would be most helpful to them; instead, we wanted to spend several days there to have a dialogue and better understand their biggest challenges. We kept hearing from the farmers that they needed more drying modules so that they could process the beans more quickly and could include more local growers in the cooperative.

For us, it was a no-brainer. We helped fund the materials and labor needed to build out 20 more drying modules dispersed throughout the region. By doing this, we knew we'd be helping the community and enabling the cooperative to produce more high-quality beans, which will better serve our members.

Our organic, whole-bean Breakfast Blend is a medium-roast coffee with flavors of dark chocolate, toffee, and caramel. We ethically source the highest quality, single-origin Arabica beans directly from a farming co-op in Peru, then roast them in small batches to ensure maximum flavor.

This grain-free and gluten-free take on granola—from nutrition coach, mom of six, and Wellne
Founder **Katie Wells**—gets its chewy, crunchy texture from a mix of coconut chips, nuts, and raisins.
Bake in the morning and serve warm or let it cool and store in an airtight container so you always have the
ultimate yogurt topping on hand.

BREAKFAST

Homemade Coconut Granola

Gluten-Free   Grain-Free   Dairy-Free   Vegan   Egg-Free

INGREDIENTS

1/4 cup Thrive Market
Organic Virgin Coconut Oil

1/4 cup Thrive Market
Organic Maple Syrup or Honey

1 teaspoon Thrive Market
Organic Vanilla Extract

2 cups Thrive Market
Organic Coconut Chips

1 cup nuts and/or seeds of
choice (try a mix of Thrive Market
Organic Cashews, Sunflower Seeds,
Pumpkin Seeds, and/or Pecans)

Pinch of Thrive Market
Organic Ground Cinnamon

1/2 cup mix of dried fruit of
choice (try Thrive Market Organic
Dried Cranberries and Apricots)

2 tablespoons Thrive Market
Organic Black Chia Seeds (optional)

INSTRUCTIONS

Preheat oven to 350°F. Melt coconut oil and honey/maple syrup in a
small saucepan until it starts to bubble. Swirl in the vanilla.

In a large bowl, mix together the coconut chips, nuts, cinnamon, dried
fruit, and chia seeds.

Pour the coconut oil mixture over the dry ingredients and mix well. The
consistency will vary some depending on the honey, coconut chips, and
coconut oil you use. If there is not enough of the honey mixture to lightly
coat all of the ingredients, add slightly more melted coconut oil and
honey in equal parts.

Spread mixture on a parchment paper-lined baking dish. Bake for 15 to
20 minutes, until it starts to brown. Remove and let cool, then crumble
into pieces. Store in an airtight jar and use within 2 weeks.

*Scan here to
shop the recipe*

No one will blame you for posting a photo of this meal before eating it. Beets lend their crimson hue to this smoothie bowl, which is then topped with antioxidant-rich raspberries, pomegranate seeds, and cacao nibs to make it the ultimate superfood breakfast.

BREAKFAST

Beet-Ginger Smoothie Bowl

Gluten-Free   Grain-Free   Dairy-Free   Egg-Free

INGREDIENTS

For the Smoothie Bowl

1 raw or cooked beet, peeled and roughly chopped

1 tablespoon grated ginger

1/4 cup frozen pineapple, cubed

1/4 cup blueberries

1 cup Thrive Market Organic Coconut Water

For the Topping

Small handful of raspberries (fresh or frozen)

1/4 cup pomegranate seeds

1 teaspoon bee pollen

2 teaspoons Thrive Market Organic Cacao Nibs

2 teaspoons Thrive Market Organic Black Chia Seeds

INSTRUCTIONS

Place all of the smoothie ingredients in a high-speed blender and blend until smooth.

Pour smoothie into a bowl and top with raspberries, pomegranate seeds, bee pollen, cacao nibs, and chia seeds.

Scan here to shop the recipe

Cake for breakfast? Yes, please! This kid-friendly recipe is a delightfully gluten-free and vegan start to any morning. Apple sauce, bananas, and maple syrup provide just enough all-natural sweetness. Serve with a schmear of nut butter for a boost of protein and healthy fats.

BREAKFAST

Gluten-Free Strawberry Oatmeal Cakes

Gluten-Free   Dairy-Free   Vegan   Egg-Free

INGREDIENTS

For the Cakes

3 cups Thrive Market Organic Gluten-Free Rolled Oats

1 tablespoon Thrive Market Baking Powder

1/2 teaspoon sea salt

2 teaspoons Thrive Market Organic Ground Cinnamon

2 flax eggs (see below)

1/4 cup Thrive Market Organic Maple Syrup

2 teaspoons Thrive Market Organic Vanilla Extract

1/2 cup Thrive Market Organic Apple Sauce (unsweetened)

2 ripe bananas

1/2 cup chopped strawberries

For 1 Flax Egg

1 tablespoon Thrive Market Organic Ground Flaxseed

3 tablespoons water

INSTRUCTIONS

First, make 2 flax eggs: In a small bowl, mix together flaxseed meal and water until combined. Let sit for 5 minutes to come together.

While the flax eggs sit, make the cakes: Preheat oven to 375°F.

In a medium bowl, stir together dry ingredients. Add wet ingredients and stir until just combined.

Distribute batter evenly into muffin tin cups and bake for 10 minutes, or until set.

Scan here to shop the recipe

Few ingredients get along as well as peanut butter and chocolate. These DIY protein bars—from **Rachael DeVaux**, registered dietitian and creator of the blog Rachael's Good Eats—taste like cookie dough, but rely on wholesome ingredients like honey and PB to achieve that craveable flavor and texture.

BREAKFAST

Peanut Butter Protein Bars

Gluten-Free   Grain-Free   Dairy-Free   Egg-Free

INGREDIENTS

1 1/2 cups Thrive Market Almond Flour

1/2 cup vanilla or unflavored protein powder of choice (try Thrive Market Organic Plant Protein in Vanilla)

3/4 cup Thrive Market Organic Peanut Butter, Creamy

5 tablespoons Thrive Market Organic Honey

3 tablespoons Thrive Market Organic Almond Beverage

1/3 cup Thrive Market Organic Dark Chocolate Chips, plus extra for topping

Pinch sea salt

INSTRUCTIONS

Line an 8x8 inch baking dish with parchment paper.

Combine almond flour and protein powder in a large bowl. Stir in the peanut butter, honey, and almond milk. Mix in the chocolate chips and sea salt.

Pour batter into the prepared baking dish and flatten with a spatula. Sprinkle with additional chocolate chips.

Transfer baking dish to the freezer for 25 minutes. Once set, remove from the freezer and slice into 12 bars. Store bars in the refrigerator in an airtight container.

Scan here to shop the recipe

The coconuts we use to make our Organic Regeneratively Grown Coconut Oil are farmed in Sri Lanka, using techniques that benefit both the planet and local communities.

Lunch

Mild, delicately flaky cod is a great way to sneak seafood past picky eaters of all ages. These fish baked in a crispy, salty, buttery crust made from gluten-free chips and cornflakes.

LUNCH

Gluten-Free Fish Sticks

Gluten-Free

Egg-Free

INGREDIENTS

3 cups Thrive Market Coconut Oil or Avocado Oil Potato Chips, crushed

2 cups gluten-free cornflakes, crushed

5 tablespoons Thrive Market Organic Ghee, melted

2 pounds skinless Thrive Market Wild-Caught Atlantic Cod fillets, cut into 1-inch strips

Sea salt and pepper, to taste

Lemon slices and roughly chopped parsley, to garnish

INSTRUCTIONS

Preheat oven to 400°F and line a baking sheet with parchment paper.

In a large bowl, combine the crushed chips and cornflakes with the melted ghee and stir.

Place the cod strips about an inch apart on the baking sheet. Season with salt and coat with chip-and-cornflake mixture, pressing it down to help the mixture adhere to the fish.

Bake for 15 minutes until the crust is golden, flaky, and crisp. Sprinkle with parsley and serve with lemon slices.

Scan here to shop the recipe

In this twist on traditional bánh mì, seared ahi tuna takes the place of pork as the protein of cho
Tuck thinly sliced steaks into gluten-free baguettes and top with a generous helping of quick-pickled
vegetables for bright, briny flavor in each bite.

LUNCH

Gluten-Free Bánh Mì With Seared Ahi Tuna

Gluten-Free   Egg-Free   Nut-Free

INGREDIENTS

For the Pickled Vegetables

3 tablespoons Thrive Market
Organic Rice Vinegar

1 teaspoon Thrive Market
Organic Honey

1/2 teaspoon Thrive Market
Organic Garlic Powder

1/2 teaspoon sea salt

1 Persian cucumber, thinly sliced

1 large carrot, shredded

1/2 small red onion, thinly sliced

1 small jalapeño, thinly sliced

For the Sauce

1/2 cup Thrive Market
Vegan Mayonnaise

1 teaspoon organic red sriracha

For the Tuna

2 (4-ounce) ahi tuna steaks; try Thrive
Market Wild-Caught Ahi Tuna

Sea salt

Thrive Market Organic
Ground Pepper, to taste

1 tablespoon Thrive Market
Organic Extra Virgin Olive Oil

For the Sandwiches

1 gluten-free baguette (or roll of
your choice), sliced lengthwise

Cilantro leaves, for serving

INSTRUCTIONS

First, make the pickled vegetables: Whisk rice vinegar, honey, garlic powder, and salt in a medium bowl. Add cucumbers, carrots, onions, and jalapeño; toss to coat.

Make the sauce: Whisk mayonnaise and sriracha in a small bowl.

Make the tuna: Season tuna with salt and pepper on both sides. Heat a large nonstick skillet over high heat and add 1 tablespoon oil. Add tuna and sear on both sides; 1 to 2 minutes total for rare, or 3 to 4 minutes total for medium-well. Transfer tuna to a cutting board and slice against the grain into 1/2-inch pieces.

Make the sandwiches: Preheat broiler. Arrange bread on a sheet tray and toast for 2 minutes, or until slightly golden. Spread sauce on one half of the bread, then layer slices of tuna on top.

Top with pickled vegetables, cilantro leaves, and another drizzle of sauce. Top with the remaining half of bread; slice and serve.

*Scan here to
shop the recipe*

Skip the drive-thru and make chicken nuggets that kiddos and their health-conscious parents will enjoy. This healthy take skips the mystery meat in favor of ground chicken and uses wholesome ingredients like flaxseed and coconut flour to create that must-have crispy coating.

LUNCH

Paleo Chicken Nuggets

Gluten-Free   Grain-Free   Dairy-Free

INGREDIENTS

1/2 cup Thrive Market Organic Coconut Flour, divided

2 tablespoons Thrive Market Organic Ground Flaxseed

1 1/4 teaspoon sea salt, divided

1 pound ground chicken

1 large egg, beaten

1 teaspoon Thrive Market Organic Onion Powder

3/4 teaspoon minced garlic

1/2 teaspoon black pepper

1/4 cup Thrive Market Organic Extra Virgin Olive Oil or Thrive Market Organic Ghee, melted

INSTRUCTIONS

Preheat oven to 375°F and line a baking sheet with parchment paper.

On a medium-sized plate, combine 1/4 cup coconut flour, ground flaxseed, and 1/4 teaspoon sea salt. Set aside.

Place ground chicken, egg, remaining 1/4 cup coconut flour, remaining 1 teaspoon sea salt, onion powder, minced garlic, and black pepper together in a large bowl and mix to combine (don't overmix).

Scoop out 1 1/2 tablespoon-sized balls. Flatten each ball into a small patty in the palm of your hand. Dip each nugget into the coconut flour mixture, coating each side, and place on baking sheet.

Bake for 15 minutes. Remove from the oven, brush each nugget with melted ghee or olive oil on both sides, and return to the oven to bake for 5 more minutes.

Serve warm with your choice of dip (try Thrive Market Ranch Dressing & Marinade).

Scan here to shop the recipe

These lightened-up chickpea patties get started on the stovetop and finished in the oven, givi crunchy outer layer usually achieved with deep-frying, only with less mess. They're wonderfully addicu on their own or as the main component of a simple pita sandwich, with parsley, cucumbers, cabbage, and yogurt sauce.

LUNCH

Chickpea Falafel

Gluten-Free   Dairy-Free   Vegan   Egg-Free

INGREDIENTS

1 cup Thrive Market Almond Flour, packed

1 pouch Thrive Market Organic Chickpeas, mashed (or 1 14.5-ounce can)

1/3 cup plus 2 tablespoons Thrive Market Organic Tahini

3 tablespoons Thrive Market Organic Coconut Aminos (or soy sauce)

1 large onion, finely diced

2 carrots, peeled and finely diced

1 bunch parsley, chopped

Juice of 2 lemons

1/2 teaspoon lemon zest

1 teaspoon Thrive Market Organic Garlic Powder

1 teaspoon Thrive Market Organic Ground Cumin

1/4 teaspoon Thrive Market Organic Ground Cinnamon

1/4 teaspoon Thrive Market Organic Cayenne Pepper

1 tablespoon sumac (optional)

INSTRUCTIONS

Preheat oven to 350°F and line a baking sheet with parchment paper.

Place all ingredients in a bowl and stir to combine. Form the mixture into patties about 2 inches wide.

Warm a drizzle of oil in a skillet over medium heat. Working in batches, cook patties for 2 minutes on each side, until browned and crispy. Transfer patties to the prepared baking sheet. Bake for 5 minutes until cooked through.

Scan here to shop the recipe

The secret to truly tasty kale salads? Massage the leaves with a little oil and salt. The process tenderizes kale leaves by breaking down their tough cellulose structure. In this recipe, massaged kale forms a nutrient-packed base for a dairy-free take on the classic Caesar salad. Nutritional yeast mimics the umami flavor of Parmesan, and crispy bacon adds extra savoriness.

LUNCH

Kale Caesar Salad

Gluten-Free　　Grain-Free　　Dairy-Free　　Egg-Free　　Nut-Free

INGREDIENTS

For the Salad

2 bunches Tuscan kale, stalks removed and discarded, leaves sliced or torn into pieces

2 tablespoons Thrive Market Organic Extra Virgin Olive Oil

Large pinch sea salt

4 strips Thrive Market Non-GMO No Sugar Added Uncured Bacon, cooked until crispy

1 avocado, peeled, pitted, and sliced

1/2 small red onion, thinly sliced

1 tablespoon Thrive Market Nutritional Yeast

For the Paleo Caesar Dressing

1 (2-ounce) can or 7 to 8 fillets anchovies, drained

2 cloves garlic

3 tablespoons Thrive Market Nutritional Yeast

1/2 teaspoon Thrive Market Organic Dijon Mustard

Juice of 1 1/2 lemons

1/4 cup vegan mayonnaise

Thrive Market Organic Ground Pepper, to taste

INSTRUCTIONS

First, massage the kale: Place the kale leaves in a large bowl. Drizzle with olive oil and a pinch of salt. Massage the kale for about 3 minutes. The leaves will shrink a little and appear darker in color.

Next, make the dressing: Place all the ingredients except the pepper in the bowl of a small food processor. Process until smooth and season to taste with pepper.

Assemble the salad: Drizzle the dressing over the kale and toss. Top the dressed salad with crumbled bacon, avocado, red onion, and nutritional yeast.

Scan here to shop the recipe

Grecian Gold

When Jeremiah McElwee first tasted a sample of what would become Thrive Market's Organic Extra Virgin Olive Oil, he was pretty certain he'd discovered the best olive oil in the world. But flavor alone wasn't enough. If he was going to offer this olive oil to Thrive Market's members, he needed to get the whole story firsthand.

First of all, why olive oil? When you see pictures of people's kitchens around the world, there's always an oil on the shelf. Oils are in every pantry in every household worldwide. Everyone uses fat to cook with, and olive oil is right at the top of the list.

When we were building out the Thrive Market line, I was very passionate. I told Thrive Market Co-Founder and CEO Nick Green, *We've got to have the olive oil that is the best our members have ever tasted.*

Thrive Market has high standards for all the products it creates and carries. What were some of the most important factors when it came to olive oil? Fraud is a big issue with olive oil, so knowing and having a connection to the source was important for us. That's how we approach everything at Thrive Market. We want to see the farms and verify that the product will be from the same place every time.

We wanted a single-origin olive oil, and to have transparency into the supply chain. You can just buy a certain grade of olive oil, but there's no way to know where it came from because it's mixed from a variety of sources. Olive oil is often refined and processed to get a consistent product. When that happens, you lose out on that natural variation. The average person might not notice the difference, but we love single-origin olive oil for the incredible, fresh, vibrant experience it provides.

So you learned of this particular olive farm in Crete. What makes their olive oil so good?
It's a family farm run by a father and his three sons, who are third-generation olive farmers. All their trees are organic, and they don't use any pesticides or GMOs. They do one harvest a year, and it's a giant celebration, a cultural tradition that brings the whole community together. They harvest the olives and press them right away, when they're fresh. Then they put the oil into these airtight, stainless steel drums and bring it to this incredible facility they've built over the years. The drums get plugged directly into a bottling line, so the oil never touches oxygen or plastic after it goes into the drums. This process results in a pristine, super-fresh product.

You went to Crete to see for yourself how their olive oil is made. What were some personal highlights of the visit? The trip was an amazing whirlwind. We went through the countryside and saw all the olive groves. Right down the road from the facility is this little seafood restaurant on the Mediterranean. I'm plant-based, and they made every traditional Greek dish vegan for me.

What are some qualities of Thrive Market's Organic Extra Virgin Olive Oil that stand out?
I remember when I first tried it. I poured some onto this little white plate, and it was this beautiful, bright, vibrant green. The smell was earthy and buttery. It was the freshest olive oil I'd ever seen or tasted.

When did you know you'd found the perfect olive oil for Thrive Market's line? At the end of my visit, the patriarch of the family said he wanted to take me to the airport. He doesn't speak any English, and I don't speak Greek. We get to the airport and he grabs me by the shoulders and starts going on and on in Greek. He was very serious—he almost seemed angry! I'm thinking, oh no, what did I do? He's probably upset that his wife had to make me vegan food. Then the translator said, the father says that having you here was a true delight, and that you have to come back and bring your whole family and stay with his family at their house. It was such a sweet moment. At that point we were all convinced. We were all in on this olive oil.

Made from 100% certified organic Koroneiki olives, our extra-virgin olive oil is grown, harvested, and bottled on a single, family-run estate in western Crete.

With pantry staples like canned wild salmon and basic spices, this elegant dish is deceptively ea
Bell peppers, shallots, and fresh parsley add a bit of brightness, while a creamy spiced remoulade brings
the flavor and flair. Serve with crackers or a leafy green salad for a light yet satisfying lunch.

LUNCH

Salmon Cakes

Gluten-Free   Grain-Free

INGREDIENTS

For the Salmon Cakes

1 (6-ounce) can wild-caught
salmon, drained

1/2 medium shallot, minced

1/2 roasted red bell pepper,
finely chopped

1 garlic clove, minced

1 egg

1 (4.25-ounce) box almond flour
crackers, crushed and divided

1/3 cup mayonnaise

1 tablespoon parsley leaves,
finely chopped

1 teaspoon Thrive Market
Organic Capers, finely chopped

1/2 teaspoon sea salt

1/4 teaspoon Thrive Market
Organic Ground Pepper

2 to 3 tablespoons Thrive
Market Organic Ghee

For the Remoulade
1/2 cup mayonnaise

Juice of 1 lime

1 tablespoon Thrive Market
Organic Stone Ground Mustard

1 tablespoon parsley,
finely chopped

1/2 teaspoon sea salt

1/2 teaspoon Thrive Market
Organic Ground Pepper

1/2 teaspoon organic red sriracha

INSTRUCTIONS

First, make the salmon cakes: Add salmon to a large mixing bowl and
break up large chunks with a fork. Add shallot, bell pepper, garlic, egg,
1/2 cup crushed crackers, mayonnaise, parsley, capers, salt, and pepper.
Stir until well blended.

Pack salmon into a 1/4-cup measuring cup; tap it into your hand to form
a patty, place the patty on sheet tray, and continue with the remaining
mixture. Add remaining crackers to a plate and dredge each salmon
cake on both sides.

Melt 2 tablespoons ghee in a large nonstick sauté pan over medium-
high heat. Add patties and gently push down with the back of a spatula
to flatten slightly. Cook for 2 to 3 minutes, or until bottom is golden;
flip and reduce heat to medium. Cook on second side for another 3 to
4 minutes.

To make the remoulade, whisk all ingredients in a small bowl and serve
alongside salmon cakes.

*Scan here to
shop the recipe*

Got leftover chicken in the fridge? Give it new life by tucking it into hearty, flavorful flautas. **Jeannette Ogden**, aka *@shutthekaleup*, took her mother's recipe and tweaked it with grain-free tortillas and nut-based cheese. You can easily substitute these ingredients to suit your diet and tastes.

LUNCH

Grain-Free Flautas

Gluten-Free   Grain-Free   Dairy-Free   Egg-Free   Nut-Free

INGREDIENTS

1/3 cup Thrive Market Avocado Oil

18 grain-free tortillas of your choice

1 whole chicken (about 2 pounds), cooked and shredded

1/2 a head of romaine lettuce, shredded

2 cups cheese of your choice (can use dairy-free)

1 bunch fresh cilantro, de-stemmed

1 jar Thrive Market Organic Salsa

INSTRUCTIONS

Lightly coat 1 skillet with oil over medium heat; you'll use this pan to warm up the tortillas before filling and rolling them. Meanwhile, add about 1/4 cup of avocado oil to another pan over medium heat; you'll use this pan to fry the flautas.

Warm the tortillas 2 at a time, 1 layered on top of the other. Be careful not to leave them in the pan too long; you want them to stay soft.

Remove the warmed tortillas from the pan and add a small handful of shredded chicken. Roll tightly and place into the frying skillet. Cook until golden and crispy, 3 to 4 minutes per side. Repeat with all the remaining tortillas.

To serve, top flautas with romaine lettuce, cheese, cilantro, and salsa as desired.

Scan here to shop the recipe

In **Dr. Mark Hyman**'s verdant take on shakshuka, aromatic herbs and a garden of green vegetables stand in for the traditional tomato sauce. To maximize nutrients and support humane farming practices, Dr. Hyman recommends using pasture-raised eggs if you can.

LUNCH

Green Shakshuka

Gluten-Free   Grain-Free   Dairy-Free   Nut-Free

INGREDIENTS

2 tablespoons Thrive Market Organic Extra Virgin Olive Oil

1 large leek, finely chopped

2 large shallots, finely chopped

2 small fennel bulbs, finely chopped

1 bunch Swiss chard, de-stemmed and roughly chopped

1 bunch spinach, de-stemmed and roughly chopped

4 kale leaves, de-stemmed and roughly chopped

3 large garlic cloves, thinly sliced

1 large zucchini, finely diced

Zest from 1 lemon

1/4 jalapeño (optional), thinly sliced

3/4 teaspoon sea salt

1/2 teaspoon Thrive Market Organic Whole Black Peppercorns, freshly ground

2 scallions, chopped

4 to 8 large eggs

1/4 cup filtered water

1/4 cup fresh dill

INSTRUCTIONS

Place a large skillet over medium heat and add olive oil. Add leeks, shallots, and fennel to the skillet and cook, stirring occasionally, until softened and caramelized, about 5 minutes.

Add the Swiss chard, spinach, kale, and garlic to the skillet and stir. Cover and cook for 5 minutes. Stir in zucchini, cover, and cook for another 5 minutes, until zucchini is soft. Add the lemon zest, jalapeño (if using), salt, pepper, and chopped scallions; stir.

Create a well for each egg in the middle of the shakshuka base and carefully crack one egg into each well. Cook for 2 to 3 minutes.

Pour water around the edge of the skillet, cover, and cook until egg whites are set, about 2 more minutes. Remove lid and sprinkle with chopped dill before serving.

Scan here to shop the recipe

If anyone knows how to keep it interesting (and delicious) on the Whole30® program, it's Co-Founder and CEO **Melissa Urban**. This satisfying salad uses bottled sauces as a shortcut to major flavor. No air fryer? We've included an oven method that works just as well.

LUNCH

Buffalo Chicken Salad

 Gluten-Free Grain-Free Dairy-Free Nut-Free

INGREDIENTS

1 pound boneless, skinless chicken breasts, thick sides pounded to make of even thickness

1/2 cup Whole30® Buffalo Vinaigrette

6 cups chopped romaine lettuce

1 cup thinly sliced celery

1/2 cup shredded carrot

3 to 4 tablespoons Whole30® House Ranch

1 small ripe avocado, peeled, pitted, and sliced

1 cup cherry tomatoes, halved

Freshly ground black pepper

2 teaspoons finely chopped chives

INSTRUCTIONS

In a large resealable plastic bag, combine chicken and Whole30® Buffalo Vinaigrette. Massage to coat. Seal bag and marinate in the refrigerator for at least 2 hours and up to 4 hours.

Preheat air fryer to 375°F. Remove chicken from bag; discard marinade. Add the chicken to the air fryer. Cook until chicken is no longer pink and the internal temperature is 170°F, turning once, about 15 minutes. Let stand while making the salad.

In a large bowl, combine the romaine, celery, and carrots. Add the Whole30® House Ranch; toss to combine. Divide salad among 4 serving plates.

Slice the chicken. Top the salads with sliced chicken, avocado, and cherry tomatoes. Season to taste with black pepper. Sprinkle with chives.

Oven method: Preheat oven to 350°F. Heat an oven-safe skillet over high heat for 5 minutes or until it is very hot (cast iron works well). Place the chicken on the hot skillet and cook for 1 minute, then flip and cook for 1 minute more on the other side.

Transfer the skillet to the oven and bake until no longer pink in the center, the juices run clear, and the chicken reaches an internal temperature of 165°F, 8 to 10 minutes.

Scan here to shop the recipe

THRIVE MARKET
REGENERATIVELY GROWN
ORGANIC
RAW
MACADAMIA
NUTS
NO ADDED SALT
USDA ORGANIC
THRIVE MARKET
REGENERATIVELY GROWN
ORGANIC
DRY ROASTED & SALTED
MACADAMIA
NUTS
SALTED
USDA ORGANIC

Our Organic Macadamia Nuts are regeneratively grown by a co-op of small-scale farmers in Kenya who work to restore soil health and help heal the environment.

Dinner

The mild taste of halibut is the ideal blank slate for a lemony hazelnut crust in this energizing dish from functional medicine expert **Chris Kresser**. Refreshing cucumbers and chives complete this restaurant-worthy meal perfect for dining al fresco.

DINNER

Paleo Hazelnut-Crusted Halibut

Gluten-Free   Grain-Free   Dairy-Free   Egg-Free

INGREDIENTS

1 tablespoon Thrive Market Organic Virgin Coconut Oil

Sea salt and white pepper, to taste

2 8-ounce halibut fillets

1 cup Thrive Market Vegan Mayonnaise

1 1/2 cups hazelnuts, very finely chopped

Juice of 1 lemon

Fresh chives, chopped

1 large cucumber, very thinly sliced

INSTRUCTIONS

Preheat oven to 375°F. Grease an ovenproof baking dish with coconut oil or ghee.

Salt and pepper the halibut and thoroughly coat with mayonnaise. Dredge the fillets in the chopped hazelnuts and place in the baking dish.

Bake for 15 minutes, or until the fish flakes easily with a fork. Keep a close eye while baking, as the hazelnuts can burn easily. If necessary, lower the temperature to 350°F.

Plate the cooked fillets, squeeze lemon over them, and garnish with chives. Arrange the sliced cucumber on the side.

Scan here to shop the recipe

Coconut milk brings creamy texture (sans dairy) to this spin on traditional seafood chowder. We recommend topping your bowls with crispy bacon immediately before serving for a hit of salt and smoke to balance it all out.

DINNER

Seafood Scallop Chowder

Gluten-Free   Grain-Free   Dairy-Free   Egg-Free

INGREDIENTS

1 pound scallops (try Thrive Market Wild-Caught Sea Scallops), patted dry

2 teaspoons sea salt, divided

2 teaspoons Thrive Market Organic Ground Pepper, divided

1 tablespoon Thrive Market Organic Virgin Coconut Oil

6 slices bacon, cut into cubes (try Thrive Market Non-GMO No Sugar Added Uncured Bacon)

1 medium onion, diced

2 cloves garlic, minced

1 small cauliflower, cut into small florets

1 (13.5-ounce) can Thrive Market Organic Coconut Milk, Regular

4 cups Thrive Market Organic Chicken Bone Broth

1 medium celery root, peeled and cut into 1/2-inch cubes

1 bag (30-40) shrimp, chopped (try Thrive Market Wild-Caught Peeled Shrimp)

Chopped parsley, for serving

INSTRUCTIONS

Arrange scallops on a sheet tray. Blend 1 teaspoon salt and 1 teaspoon pepper and sprinkle the mixture on both sides.

Heat coconut oil in a large Dutch oven over medium-high heat. When hot, add bacon and cook until crisp, about 3 to 5 minutes; remove with a slotted spoon to drain on a paper towel-lined plate. Add scallops to bacon fat and sear on both sides, about 1 to 2 minutes. Transfer to a plate and cool.

Add onion and garlic to the Dutch oven; sauté until soft, about 5 to 7 minutes. Stir in cauliflower, coconut milk, chicken bone broth, remaining 1 teaspoon salt, and remaining 1 teaspoon pepper to taste. Bring to a boil. Reduce heat to simmer and let cauliflower cook until tender, about 10 minutes.

Using an immersion blender, purée until smooth. (Alternatively, you can purée the soup in batches in a high-speed blender.) Add celery root and simmer until pieces are easily pierced with a fork, about 5 minutes.

Cut scallops into smaller pieces, then return them (including any juices) to the pot. Add shrimp and stir. Cook for 3 to 4 minutes, until shrimp have turned pink and curled slightly.

Sprinkle parsley on soup before serving.

Scan here to shop the recipe

A spicy-sweet marinade transforms tofu into a craveable taco filling in this lively dish from holistic health pro **Pamela Salzman**. Serve with a light and citrusy avocado crema—and maybe a margarita?

DINNER

Chipotle Tofu Tacos

Gluten-Free   Grain-Free   Dairy-Free   Vegan   Egg-Free

INGREDIENTS

1 block (12 to 15 ounces) extra-firm tofu, preferably organic/non-GMO and sprouted

For the Marinade

1 tablespoon Thrive Market Organic Extra Virgin Olive Oil

1 tablespoon Thrive Market Organic Coconut Aminos

1 tablespoon fresh orange juice

2 teaspoons Thrive Market Organic Maple Syrup

1 tablespoon arrowroot starch or Thrive Market Organic Corn Starch

1/2 teaspoon chipotle powder

1/2 teaspoon Thrive Market Organic Chili Powder

1/2 teaspoon Thrive Market Organic Garlic Powder

1/2 teaspoon Thrive Market Organic Smoked Paprika

For the Avocado-Lime Crema (optional)

1 large ripe avocado, peeled and pitted

1/2 cup Thrive Market Vegan Mayonnaise

1/2 cup cilantro leaves and tender stems

Juice of 1 lime, about 2 tablespoons

1/4 teaspoon of salt, plus more to taste

For Serving

Warm grain-free tortillas or lettuce leaves

Pickled onions (optional)

Shredded cabbage (optional)

Radishes (optional)

Thrive Market Organic Salsa (optional)

INSTRUCTIONS

Preheat oven to 400°F and line a large, rimmed baking sheet with parchment paper.

Slice the tofu in half lengthwise, wrap the blocks in paper towels, and place on a cutting board. Place something heavy (like a skillet filled with cans) on top of the tofu and allow to sit for 15 minutes or longer, if possible, to drain excess liquid. Once drained, cut tofu into 1-inch cubes.

In a medium bowl or a container that can hold the tofu in 1 layer, mix all the marinade ingredients until well combined. Add the tofu and gently coat each piece, trying not to break the cubes.

While the tofu marinates, make the crema: In a blender or the bowl of a food processor fitted with the metal S blade, combine all the crema ingredients and process until smooth, adding a tablespoon or 2 of water to thin it out if necessary.

Arrange the tofu in 1 layer on the prepared baking sheet and bake for 20 to 25 minutes, tossing halfway, until it is crispy and golden on the edges.

Fill tortillas or lettuce leaves with tofu along with crema and your choice of toppings.

Scan here to shop the recipe

Cauliflower stands in for grits in this carb-conscious version of a Southern comfort food classic, created by **Wes Shoemaker** of Highfalutin' Low Carb. With garlicky shrimp and salty bacon, this savory dish is sure to be a hit on the dinner table; it also makes an impressive brunch spread.

DINNER

Shrimp & Cauliflower "Grits"

Gluten-Free   Grain-Free   Nut-Free

INGREDIENTS

1 pound frozen cauliflower florets

3 tablespoons butter or Thrive Market Organic Ghee, divided

3 tablespoons heavy whipping cream

4 ounces gouda cheese, shredded

Salt & Thrive Market Organic Ground Pepper to taste

4 ounces diced pancetta or Thrive Market Non-GMO No Sugar Added Uncured Bacon

1 shallot, diced (or 2 tablespoons diced onion)

1 tablespoon minced garlic

1 pound Thrive Market Wild-Caught Peeled Shrimp

4–5 green onions, thinly sliced (green parts only)

Squeeze of lemon

INSTRUCTIONS

Microwave the frozen cauliflower in a covered glass bowl for 10–12 minutes, stirring occasionally. Mash with a potato masher until it is the consistency of grits. Add 1 tablespoon of butter, the heavy whipping cream, and gouda cheese. Mix well and season with salt and pepper to taste. Keep warm.

Sauté the pancetta or bacon over medium-low heat until crispy. Remove and set aside. In the remaining bacon fat, add 2 tablespoons of butter and cook the shallots or onions until lightly browned. Add the garlic and stir until fragrant, about 30 seconds.

Add the shrimp. Cook for 8 to 10 minutes or until the shrimp are just cooked and still tender. Remove from heat and mix in the reserved bacon/pancetta and scallions.

Serve the cauliflower "grits" in a shallow bowl and top generously with the shrimp and sauce. Top with a squeeze of lemon and serve.

Scan here to shop the recipe

In this rewarding departure from your average beef burger—shared by paleo expert and Primal Kitchen Founder **Mark Sisson**—vibrant pistachio pesto balances the savory flavor of lamb, while cooling mint gives each bite a fresh finish.

DINNER

Lamb Burgers With Pistachio Pesto

Gluten-Free   Grain-Free   Dairy-Free   Egg-Free

INGREDIENTS

For the Burgers

1 1/2 pounds ground lamb

1 teaspoon Thrive Market Organic Ground Cumin

1/4 teaspoon Thrive Market Organic Ground Cinnamon

1/4 teaspoon Thrive Market Organic Ground Allspice

1/2 teaspoon salt

1/4 teaspoon Thrive Market Organic Ground Pepper

1/4 cup mint leaves, finely chopped

1/4 cup parsley, chopped

For the Pistachio Pesto

1 garlic clove

1 cup Thrive Market Organic Roasted & Salted Pistachios

1/2 cup Thrive Market Avocado Oil

1 teaspoon lemon juice, or more to taste

1/4 cup mint leaves, loosely packed

Pinch of salt

INSTRUCTIONS

First, make the burgers: Mix together the ground lamb, spices, chopped mint, and parsley. Form 4 patties and pan-fry or grill them, about 4 to 6 minutes per side.

Next, make the pistachio pesto: While the burgers are cooking, blend together garlic, pistachios, avocado oil, lemon juice, whole mint leaves, and salt in a food processor. Serve burgers with pesto on top.

Scan here to shop the recipe

LES VIGNES DE COULOUS
CADILLAC CÔTES DE BORDEAUX, FRANCE

Returning to Bordeaux

Josh Nadel, Master Sommelier for Thrive Market's clean wine program, had the privilege of tasting winemaker Pauline Lapierre's first-ever vintage at a wine trade fair in Germany. He was drawn to her responsible practices and the beautiful expression of terroir in her wines, which he says "represent expertise, passion, and risk."

He hopes her approach ushers in a new guard of vintners doing things the old way. "She's paving the way for other winemakers who want to get back to the roots of winemaking and transition to organics," he says.

Here, Nadel and Lapierre talk about Pauline's journey back to Bordeaux in search of better wine and organic methods that help heal the earth.

Tell me about your connection to Bordeaux. I spent my childhood on my family's winery, Château Haut-Rian, in Bordeaux. Years later, I bought my own small plot of land just a few miles from my parents' estate. I saw it as an opportunity to train in organic farming and do my own thing.

My small estate had been farmed organically for a decade by the previous owner. My number-one priority became growing healthy grapes in a healthy environment without relying on chemicals. This is, I think, the main task of my generation.

Before starting your own winery, what were you doing with your life? In my twenties, I spent two years in Singapore working as a financial controller. During that time, I couldn't find a delicious bottle of wine at a fair price. In Singapore, 6,700 miles from France, every bottle I came across was either absurdly expensive or super industrial.

When my parents came to visit me in Singapore, they brought wine from the family estate. It was pure and fresh. The taste immediately brought me back to my childhood. That's when I knew something was missing from my life.

I realized I was just doing a job. I didn't feel any fulfillment or accomplishment. So I left my career in finance and returned to France to study oenology, the science of wine and winemaking.

What's different about your approach to wine and winemaking? When my parents founded their vineyard over 30 years ago, most winemakers believed that technology would improve everything. In contrast, my approach to winemaking involves good land management and minimal intervention between the grapes I grow and the wine you drink.

My wines get their character from the air, the gravelly soil, and the way the sun hits my southeast-facing vineyard. My grape yields are relatively low, given that the vines are up to 50 years old and I let grass grow wild around them. I exclusively use my estate-grown organic grapes, and we do everything from fermentation to bottling at my winery, Les Vignes de Coulous.

We're constantly discovering new winemakers and grape varietals to introduce to our members, which means our wine selection is constantly changing. No matter which wine we feature on **ThriveMarket.com**, know that they are produced using organic and sustainable farming practices and clean winemaking methods.

A lively medley of coriander, paprika, garlic, and cinnamon turn simple weeknight chicken into an aromatic treat for the taste buds in this recipe from **JJ Virgin**.

DINNER

Roasted Spice-Rubbed Chicken Thighs

Gluten-Free   Grain-Free   Dairy-Free   Egg-Free   Nut-Free

INGREDIENTS

1 teaspoon Thrive Market Organic Ground Coriander

1 teaspoon Thrive Market Organic Paprika

3/4 teaspoon Thrive Market Organic Garlic Powder

1/4 teaspoon Thrive Market Organic Ground Cinnamon

3/4 teaspoon sea salt

1/4 teaspoon Thrive Market Organic Ground Pepper

8 organic free range bone-in skinless chicken thighs, about 2 to 2 1/4 pounds, trimmed

1 tablespoon Thrive Market Avocado Oil or red palm fruit oil

INSTRUCTIONS

Preheat oven to 400°F. Lightly oil a large, shallow roasting pan.

Combine the coriander, paprika, garlic powder, cinnamon, salt, and pepper in a small bowl.

Toss the chicken and oil in a separate bowl. Pour the spice mixture over the chicken and toss to coat. Place chicken on the prepared roasting pan.

Roast chicken in the center of the oven until a thermometer inserted into the thickest part of the thigh registers 165°F. It should take approximately 23 to 25 minutes. Let rest 5 minutes before serving.

Scan here to shop the recipe

Poaching infuses mild, flaky cod with the fresh flavors of lemongrass, lime, and ginger. Crushed red pepper flakes and jalapeño provide a kick, which you can adjust to suit your taste.

DINNER

Ginger Cod in Lemongrass Coconut Broth

Gluten-Free   Grain-Free   Dairy-Free   Egg-Free

INGREDIENTS

2 tablespoons Thrive Market Organic Virgin Coconut Oil

1 large shallot, minced

3 garlic cloves, roughly chopped

1/2 teaspoon Thrive Market Organic Crushed Red Pepper

1 (14.5-ounce) can Thrive Market Organic Coconut Milk

1 cup vegetable broth

2 (4-inch) stalks lemongrass, halved lengthwise and smashed

Peels and juice from 2 limes

1 (2-inch) piece ginger, peeled and thinly sliced

2 teaspoons fish sauce

2 sprigs fresh cilantro, plus more for garnish

4 (4-ounce) boneless, skinless Thrive Market Wild-Caught Atlantic Cod fillets

1 teaspoon sea salt

1/4 teaspoon Thrive Market Organic Ground Pepper

1 jalapeño, thinly sliced, for garnish

INSTRUCTIONS

Add coconut oil to a large skillet and warm over medium heat. When melted, add shallot, garlic, and red pepper flakes; sauté until shallot is translucent, about 2 to 3 minutes.

Add coconut milk, vegetable broth, lemongrass, lime peels, ginger, fish sauce, and cilantro. Simmer, whisking occasionally, for 2 minutes.

Lightly place the fish into the sauce and bring sauce back to a simmer, then cover the pan and reduce heat to low. Cook about 5 to 6 minutes, or until cod is cooked through and flaky.

Transfer fish to a shallow bowl. Whisk lime juice, salt, and pepper into the sauce, then ladle it over the fish. Garnish with cilantro and jalapeño.

Scan here to shop the recipe

To maximize the nutrients in your diet, the more colors on your plate, the better. Kids will love eating the rainbow with this many-hued, vegetable-forward bowl created by Dr. Mikhail Varshavski, better known as **Doctor Mike**.

DINNER

Rainbow Bowl With Sautéed Chicken

 Gluten-Free   Dairy-Free   Egg-Free

INGREDIENTS

For the Bowl

1/2 cup Thrive Market Organic Sprouted Quinoa

1 cup chicken or vegetable stock

1 tablespoon Thrive Market Organic Extra Virgin Olive Oil

1 clove garlic, minced

1 chicken breast, cubed

1/4 teaspoon Thrive Market Organic Garlic Powder

Salt and pepper, to taste

1/4 cup diced onion

1/2 large carrot, shredded

1/2 cup sliced cherry tomatoes

1/2 cup shredded red cabbage

1/4 cup shelled edamame, steamed

1/2 avocado, peeled, pitted, and sliced

Fresh scallions

Sesame seeds

Cilantro

For the Dressing

2 tablespoons gluten-free soy sauce or Thrive Market Organic Coconut Aminos

1 teaspoon Thrive Market Organic Honey

1/4 teaspoon sesame oil

1 clove garlic, minced

INSTRUCTIONS

Cook quinoa in chicken or vegetable stock according to package instructions and set aside.

In a saucepan over medium heat, add olive oil and sauté 1 clove of minced garlic. Once lightly browned, add cubed chicken, garlic powder, salt, and pepper to taste and sauté until fully cooked.

In a small bowl, make the dressing by whisking together soy sauce or coconut aminos, honey, sesame oil, and remaining garlic. Set aside.

Assemble the bowl(s): Start with a scoop of cooked quinoa, then add chicken, onion, carrots, cherry tomatoes, cabbage, and edamame. Top with sliced avocado, scallions, cilantro, and sesame seeds as desired. Drizzle with dressing and serve.

Scan here to shop the recipe

Thinly sliced beef tip steak, diced bell peppers, and mixed greens form a primal trifecta in this warm salad created by **Robb Wolf**, author of *The Paleo Solution* and *Wired to Eat.* We recommend topping this hearty mix with a drizzle of balsamic vinegar.

DINNER

Stir-Fry Beef Salad

Gluten-Free Grain-Free Dairy-Free Egg-Free

INGREDIENTS

2 teaspoons Thrive Market Organic Extra Virgin Olive Oil

3/4 cup sliced onion

1 pound beef tip steak, sliced into thin strips

1 tablespoon Thrive Market Organic Coconut Aminos

1 to 2 cups sliced bell peppers

1 bag of mixed greens

Balsamic vinegar, to serve

INSTRUCTIONS

Add olive oil to a skillet over medium heat. Add sliced onions and sauté for about 5 minutes, until soft.

Add the beef and the coconut aminos and cook, tossing frequently, for about 5 minutes or until beef has browned.

Add the bell peppers and cook for a few minutes, until your desired texture is reached (longer for softer peppers, less time if you want more crunch).

Arrange mixed greens on plates, then top with the stir-fry mixture. Drizzle with balsamic vinegar and more olive oil to taste.

Scan here to shop the recipe

This easy and impressive dinner for two feels celebratory, making it equally appropriate for date night or a regular Tuesday. It calls for a splash of white wine, so grab a couple of glasses and enjoy a sip while you cook.

DINNER

Pork Chops With Creamy Mushroom Sauce

 Gluten-Free   Grain-Free   Egg-Free   Nut-Free

INGREDIENTS

2 (1 1/4-inch thick) bone-in pork rib chops

1 1/2 teaspoons sea salt, divided

1/2 teaspoon Thrive Market Organic Garlic Powder

1/2 teaspoon Thrive Market Organic Thyme

1/4 teaspoon Thrive Market Organic Ground Pepper

3 tablespoons unsalted butter, divided

8 ounces cremini mushrooms, sliced

1/4 cup dry white wine

1/2 cup heavy cream

1/2 cup Thrive Market Organic Chicken Bone Broth

2 tablespoons cream cheese

2 tablespoons parsley, chopped

INSTRUCTIONS

Preheat oven to 350°F and season pork chops with 1 teaspoon salt, garlic powder, thyme, and pepper. Add 1 tablespoon butter to a cast iron skillet set over medium-high heat. Sear pork chops for 4 minutes per side, until a golden crust forms. Transfer pork to a plate.

To the same pan, add remaining 2 tablespoons butter and mushrooms, arranging them in a single layer. Let mushrooms caramelize (resist the urge to stir at this stage), about 3 to 4 minutes. Add remaining 1/2 teaspoon salt, stir, and cook for 2 minutes more. Add wine and let it reduce for 2 to 3 minutes, then add the heavy cream and chicken broth.

Add cream cheese and whisk until incorporated. Simmer sauce until slightly thickened, about 3 to 5 minutes. Return chops to the pan and reduce heat to low. Baste the chops with sauce and simmer 2 to 3 minutes, then place the pan in the oven and cook for about 5 minutes, or until the internal temperature of the pork chops reaches 145 to 150°F. Let stand for 5 minutes before slicing. Sprinkle with parsley and serve.

Scan here to shop the recipe

Meat Matters

Mike Hacaga is the Lead Product Innovator for Thrive Market Meat & Seafood. We spoke to him about his first (of many) trips to visit our grass-fed beef partner in Patagonia.

How are cattle raised differently in Chile as compared to the U.S.? In Patagonia, the beef industry is connected to its roots. The land and cattle are tended by huasos, or Chilean cowboys, who favor a natural and humane approach. This is a far cry from the modern factory farming practiced worldwide.

The huasos expertly move the cattle across the prairies, from one fresh parcel of green grass to another, using nothing more than a horse, a whistle, and a couple of herding dogs. In comparison, herders in the U.S. often use ATVs.

When you watch them herd the cattle, it's nothing less than poetry in motion. The dogs don't nip at the cattle's heels; instead, they wait patiently at the horse's front hoof, looking up at their huaso and awaiting a command. The dogs use their training and their natural herding instincts to move the animals in perfect synchrony.

Unlike cows in the U.S., these Chilean cows aren't fearful because they've never been mishandled or mistreated. The animals are curious and more than willing to approach a perfect stranger like myself.

Eating pasture-raised, grass-fed beef—instead of the industrially raised, grain-fed beef most of us in the U.S. have become accustomed to—is a crucial choice. It's not only better for your own nutrition and well-being; it's better for the future health of the ranchers, their animals, and the planet.

Why do you want members to have access to grass-fed beef as opposed to grain-fed? For the majority of my life, I admittedly wasn't a huge fan of the flavor and texture of grass-fed beef. But my opinion changed during my first visit to Chile. At night, the ranchers barbecued beef and lamb over a wood-burning fire in the pasture, overlooking a beautiful lake. I kid you not, this was unlike any other grass-fed beef I had tasted. It was tender and had a rich, deep, robust beef flavor.

But it's not just the flavor. The ranchers have successfully married old-world techniques with new learnings, resulting in a perfect balance between sustainability, animal welfare, and regenerative agriculture. Witnessing this harmony keeps me hopeful about the future.

What is the future of sustainably raised and harvested beef? That future includes setting a new benchmark for the beef Americans feed their families. By bringing this incredible product to Thrive Market members, I can give people access to beef that is of higher quality and better provenance than anything I've found in my 30 years in the industry.

Our G.A.P. Certified, 100% grass-fed beef comes from Patagonia, Chile, where ranchers prioritize animal welfare and sustainability. For every cow that's harvested, a native tree is planted.

In this hearty recipe, jarred tomato sauce is a shortcut that tastes anything but. Serve these juicy, flavorful meatballs with pasta, zucchini noodles, or however you wish—with fresh mozzarella and chopped basil, you really can't go wrong.

DINNER

Baked Meatballs With Fresh Mozzarella

Gluten-Free   Grain-Free   Nut-Free

INGREDIENTS

1 pound Thrive Market Grass-Fed Ground Beef

1 cup grated shallots, squeezed and drained of their juices

2 egg yolks

2 tablespoons chopped parsley

3 tablespoons chopped chives

1/4 teaspoon Thrive Market Organic Ground Allspice

1/2 teaspoon Thrive Market Organic Garlic Powder

1 teaspoon Thrive Market Organic Ground Cumin

2 teaspoons sea salt

Zest of 2 lemons

1 tablespoon Thrive Market Organic Extra Virgin Olive Oil

1 jar Thrive Market Organic Pasta Sauce, Tomato Basil

1 cup fresh mozzarella, sliced

1/4 cup fresh basil, for garnish

INSTRUCTIONS

Preheat oven to 350°F.

Place beef, shallots, egg yolks, parsley, chives, allspice, garlic powder, cumin, salt, and lemon zest in a large bowl and mix together with a fork until just combined. Shape into 1-inch meatballs.

Heat olive oil in a large ovenproof skillet. Brown meatballs on all sides. Pour tomato sauce over meatballs. Place skillet in the oven and allow meatballs to cook through, about 8 minutes.

Remove the skillet from the oven and arrange sliced mozzarella over the top. Place under the broiler for 5 minutes until cheese is melted and bubbly.

Let cool slightly and top with fresh basil before serving.

Scan here to shop the recipe

Fig preserves and sriracha sauce may strike you as an unlikely combination, but they pair beautifully in this simple salmon recipe from holistic health expert **Pamela Salzman**. No fig preserves on hand? Salzman says apricot also works.

DINNER

Herbed Sweet & Spicy Salmon

 Gluten-Free
 Grain-Free
 Dairy-Free
 Egg-Free
 Nut-Free

INGREDIENTS

1 (24-ounce) Wild-Caught Salmon fillet (skin-on or skinless)

2 teaspoons Thrive Market Organic Extra Virgin Olive Oil

3/4 teaspoon sea salt

Thrive Market Organic Ground Pepper

3 tablespoons no-sugar-added fig preserves (or other fruit preserves; try Thrive Market Organic Apricot Fruit Spread)

3/4 teaspoon organic red sriracha

1 cup mixed fresh tender green herbs, finely chopped (try flat-leaf parsley, mint, dill, or any combination)

INSTRUCTIONS

Preheat oven to 425°F. Line a rimmed baking sheet with parchment paper.

Place the salmon on the prepared baking sheet. Drizzle the salmon with olive oil and rub to coat evenly. Sprinkle with salt and pepper.

In a small bowl, combine the preserves and the sriracha. Spread a thin layer of the mixture on the salmon. Press the herb mixture on top of the salmon to cover evenly.

Roast the salmon for 10 to 12 minutes, or until fish flakes evenly when poked with the tip of a paring knife. You want the fish to be slightly rare in the center. Cut crosswise into pieces and serve immediately.

Scan here to shop the recipe

Few things say "comfort food" like a bowl of pasta with sauce. This plant-rich version—from vegan chef **Caitlin Shoemaker**, aka *@frommybowl*—requires only five main ingredients, but you can also toss in some fresh greens or roasted vegetables to make it your own.

DINNER

Vegan Roasted Red Pepper Pasta

Dairy-Free   Vegan   Egg-Free

INGREDIENTS

Sea salt

8 ounces pasta of choice (try Thrive Market Organic Biodynamic Whole Wheat Spaghetti)

1 12-ounce jar or 14.5-ounce can roasted red peppers, drained and rinsed (can also use 8 ounces homemade)

2 cloves garlic

1 cup Thrive Market Organic Coconut Milk

1/2 cup vegetable broth

1/4 teaspoon Thrive Market Organic Crushed Red Pepper (optional)

INSTRUCTIONS

Bring a large pot of salted water to a boil and cook the pasta according to the package instructions.

In the meantime, add the peppers, garlic, coconut milk, vegetable broth, and red chili flakes (optional) to a blender. Blend on high for 45 to 60 seconds, until the sauce is smooth and creamy. Season with salt and pepper to taste, if necessary.

Drain the pasta once cooked, but do not rinse. Return the empty pot to the stovetop and add the red pepper sauce. Bring the sauce to a simmer over medium-high heat and cook for 2 to 3 minutes, until bubbly and thickened.

Remove the pot from heat and add the cooked pasta. Toss pasta with sauce using tongs. If the sauce appears runny, allow the pasta to sit for an additional 3 to 5 minutes to absorb more of it.

Transfer the pasta into bowls and serve.

Scan here to shop the recipe

In this recipe, steaming with bone broth keeps the chicken extraordinarily tender, while allowing the
to soak up all the bold flavor that fresh ginger, garlic, and green chiles have to offer. Bonus: easy cleanup.

DINNER

One-Pot Chile-Ginger Chicken & Rice

Gluten-Free   Dairy-Free   Egg-Free

INGREDIENTS

3 cups Thrive Market Organic
Chicken Bone Broth

6 large slices ginger, cut lengthwise

4 cloves garlic, peeled and halved

1 long green chile, such as
Anaheim or Hatch, sliced

1 1/2 cups Thrive Market
Organic White Jasmine Rice

4 small boneless skinless
chicken thighs

1 teaspoon sea salt

Thrive Market Organic
Ground Pepper

1 bunch scallions, sliced

1 cup cilantro, roughly chopped

INSTRUCTIONS

Stir chicken broth, ginger, garlic, and chile together in a 3 1/2-quart
Dutch oven or another deep pan with high sides. Bring to a boil over
medium heat, then add rice and stir. Bring to a boil again, then add
chicken and season with salt and pepper.

Cover, turn heat down to low, and cook for 20 minutes. At this point,
the rice should have absorbed all liquid and chicken should be tender.
Top with scallions and cilantro. Serve with coconut aminos on the side.

*Scan here to
shop the recipe*

Zippy and herbaceous, our Green Goddess Dressing & Marinade is made with MCT oil for a dose of healthy fats.

Snacks & Sides

These are tots like you've never had them: baked, not fried, and bursting with nutritious broccoli and cauliflower. A flavorful blend of spices and a bright and citrusy mayo dipping sauce (that comes together in no time thanks to a few shortcuts) make them borderline addictive.

SNACKS & SIDES

Veggie Tots

Gluten-Free Grain-Free Dairy-Free

INGREDIENTS

For the Veggie Tots

Thrive Market Avocado Oil Spray (can also use coconut oil spray)

2 cups cauliflower florets

1 cup broccoli florets

1 egg white

1 tablespoon avocado oil mayo

1/2 cup Thrive Market Almond Flour

1/4 cup fresh parsley leaves

1 teaspoon sea salt

1/4 teaspoon Thrive Market Organic Garlic Powder

1/2 teaspoon Thrive Market Organic Onion Powder

1/4 teaspoon Thrive Market Organic Ground Pepper

For the Dipping Sauce

1/4 cup mayonnaise; try Thrive Market Vegan Mayonnaise or Coconut Oil Mayonnaise

2 tablespoons premade citrus vinaigrette of your choice (can also use homemade)

INSTRUCTIONS

Preheat oven to 400°F. Line a baking sheet with parchment paper and mist with oil spray.

Place cauliflower and broccoli in a food processor and pulse until the mixture is the consistency of rice. Add egg white, mayonnaise, almond flour, parsley, salt, garlic powder, onion powder, and black pepper. Pulse until fully blended.

Scoop the mixture using a tablespoon and form into oval-shaped patties between your palms; place on the prepared baking sheet. Repeat with remaining mixture. Bake for 20 minutes in the top rack of the oven, rotating the sheet halfway through.

While the tots cook, whisk mayo and dressing in a small bowl. Serve alongside veggie tots.

Scan here to shop the recipe

Inspired by the Mexican street food staple, this flavorful (and delightfully messy) elote stars creamy mayonnaise, crumbly feta, and plenty of fresh lime.

SNACKS & SIDES

Grilled Corn With Chipotle-Lime Mayonnaise

Gluten-Free   Grain-Free

INGREDIENTS

6 ears of corn, husked

1 cup Thrive Market Coconut Oil Mayonnaise

1 cup crumbled feta cheese

Zest of 2 limes

1/3 cup chopped cilantro

2 limes, sliced, to serve

INSTRUCTIONS

Heat grill to medium. Place corn on grill and cook until kernels begin to char, 3 to 5 minutes. Turn ears and repeat until cooked on all sides.

Remove corn from grill, slather with mayo, and roll in feta cheese to coat on all sides. Sprinkle with lime zest and cilantro. Serve with lime wedges.

Scan here to shop the recipe

If plant-based eating has you nostalgic for bacon, you're in luck. This recipe transforms coconut f
salty, smoky, bacon-like bits that are delicious sprinkled over a salad, tucked into a baked potato, or —
why not?—on a maple-flavored donut. Make sure to use unsweetened coconut.

SNACKS & SIDES

4-Ingredient Vegan Coconut Bacon

Gluten-Free   Grain-Free   Dairy-Free   Vegan   Egg-Free

INGREDIENTS

3 cups Thrive Market
Organic Coconut Chips

4 tablespoons Thrive Market
Organic Coconut Aminos

2 tablespoons liquid smoke

Drizzle of Thrive Market
Organic Maple Syrup

INSTRUCTIONS

Preheat oven to 350°F. Line a baking sheet with parchment paper.

In a bowl, combine all ingredients until coconut chips are completely coated. Transfer the coconut chips to the baking sheet in an even layer.

Bake for 12 to 14 minutes, tossing occasionally. Let cool, then store in the fridge for up to 7 days or in the freezer indefinitely.

*Scan here to
shop the recipe*

In **Chris Kresser**'s lightened-up version of a classic steakhouse side, coconut milk takes the place of whole milk and heavy cream, while a pinch of nutmeg warms up each bite.

SNACKS & SIDES

Creamed Collard Greens

Gluten-Free   Grain-Free   Dairy-Free   Egg-Free

INGREDIENTS

1 tablespoon Thrive Market
Regenerative Pork Fat

1 pound collard greens,
washed and cut into large pieces

1 cup Thrive Market
Organic Coconut Milk

1 tablespoon Thrive Market
Organic Coconut Aminos

Pinch of Thrive Market
Organic Ground Nutmeg

Sea salt and freshly ground
pepper, to taste

Hazelnuts, roasted and
chopped for garnish (optional)

INSTRUCTIONS

Melt fat in a sauté pan and add all the ingredients except optional hazelnuts (if using). Cook at medium-high heat for 10 minutes or until the liquid has greatly reduced. Add salt to taste.

Garnish with chopped hazelnuts, if using, and serve.

*Scan here to
shop the recipe*

Warm, savory cumin and paprika balance out the naturally caramelized flavor of sweet potato in these crunchy baked chips—which are just as addictive as the bagged variety, but a lot more wholesome.

SNACKS & SIDES

Cumin-Spiced Sweet Potato Chips

Gluten-Free   Grain-Free   Dairy-Free   Vegan   Egg-Free

INGREDIENTS

1 large sweet potato, peeled

2 tablespoons Thrive Market Organic Virgin Coconut Oil, melted

2 teaspoons Thrive Market Organic Ground Cumin

Pinch Thrive Market Organic Paprika

1 1/2 teaspoons salt

INSTRUCTIONS

Preheat oven to 400°F. Line a baking sheet with parchment paper.

Using a mandoline or sharp knife, slice sweet potato into very thin rounds. Place in a large bowl and toss with coconut oil, cumin, paprika, and salt.

Spread potato slices on baking sheet in a single, even layer. Bake for 20 to 25 minutes or until crisp and golden brown. Let cool fully before enjoying; chips will firm up slightly as they cool.

Scan here to shop the recipe

Naturally creamy avocado plus a splash of almond milk give this dip its luscious texture, while a squeeze of lime adds brightness and fresh jalapeño turns up the heat. Pair with chips (try Thrive Market Non-GMO Grain-Free Lime Tortilla Chips) or carrot sticks for a casual but crowd-pleasing appetizer.

SNACKS & SIDES

Avocado Dip With a Kick

Gluten-Free   Grain-Free   Dairy-Free   Vegan   Egg-Free

INGREDIENTS

2 ripe avocados, peeled and pitted

Zest and juice of 1 lime

1/2 jalapeño, chopped (seeds removed for less heat)

1/4 cup Thrive Market Organic Almond Beverage

1 tablespoon chopped cilantro

1 teaspoon Thrive Market Organic Garlic Powder

1/2 teaspoon sea salt

1/4 teaspoon Thrive Market Organic Ground Pepper

INSTRUCTIONS

Add all ingredients to a food processor; blend until smooth. Chill until ready to eat.

Store dip in an airtight container in the fridge for up to 5 days.

Scan here to shop the recipe

Delightfully crisp and refreshing, **JJ Virgin**'s vegan slaw will brighten up any picnic spread. Chopping accounts for most of the work—then just let the mixture hang out in a tart, herbaceous vinaigrette and absorb its flavor.

SNACKS & SIDES

Jicama, Apple & Pear Slaw

Gluten-Free   Grain-Free   Dairy-Free   Vegan   Egg-Free

INGREDIENTS

1 cup shredded red cabbage

1 cup shredded green cabbage

1 medium apple, cored and cut into matchsticks

1 medium ripe pear, cored and cut into matchsticks

1/2 small jicama, peeled and cut into matchsticks, about 1 cup

3 green onions, chopped

4 teaspoons Thrive Market Organic Apple Cider Vinegar

1 tablespoon macadamia nut oil

1 tablespoon chopped fresh cilantro

1/4 teaspoon sea salt

INSTRUCTIONS

Toss the cabbage, apple, pear, jicama, green onions, vinegar, oil, cilantro, and salt together in a large bowl. Let stand 30 minutes, tossing occasionally, to allow the flavors to develop.

Scan here to shop the recipe

If you've never thought to throw your salad on the grill, give it a try—starting with romaine hearts. The outer leaves soften and char as they cook, while the core remains crunchy. Drizzle with an avocado-lime dressing and serve warm for a showstopping salad.

SNACKS & SIDES

Grilled Romaine Salad With Avocado-Lime Dressing

Gluten-Free   Grain-Free   Nut-Free

INGREDIENTS

For the Avocado-Lime Dressing

1 avocado, peeled and pitted

1/4 cup cilantro leaves

Juice of 3 limes

Large pinch sea salt

Freshly ground pepper

1 teaspoon Thrive Market Organic Onion Powder

Small pinch Thrive Market Organic Cayenne Pepper

1/4 to 1/3 cup Thrive Market Organic Extra Virgin Olive Oil

For the Salad

6 romaine hearts, sliced lengthwise into halves

Thrive Market Organic Extra Virgin Olive Oil, for grilling

2 to 4 hard-boiled eggs, halved (optional)

Grated Parmesan cheese (optional)

INSTRUCTIONS

Heat grill to medium.

While the grill heats, make the dressing: Combine avocado, cilantro, lime juice, salt, pepper, onion powder, and cayenne in a blender or food processor and blend until smooth. Drizzle in olive oil and blend until creamy and pourable. If the dressing is too thick, add a few drops of water to thin.

Once the grill is hot, brush romaine hearts with olive oil and grill for 20 seconds on each side.

Serve warm romaine hearts drizzled with dressing and, if you like, topped with quartered eggs and grated Parmesan.

Scan here to shop the recipe

Potato chips, hold the potato (and the deep-frying). Delicate Brussels sprouts leaves turn crispy and craveable when tossed with an acidic salt-and-vinegar combo and roasted for just a few minutes.

SNACKS & SIDES

Salt & Vinegar Brussels Sprouts Chips

Gluten-Free   Grain-Free   Dairy-Free   Vegan   Egg-Free   Nut-Free

INGREDIENTS

1 pound Brussels sprouts

2 tablespoons Thrive Market Organic Extra Virgin Olive Oil

1 tablespoon Thrive Market Organic Apple Cider Vinegar

1/2 teaspoon Thrive Market Pink Himalayan Salt

INSTRUCTIONS

Preheat oven to 350°F. Line a baking sheet with parchment paper.

Cut off the bottom of each sprout to remove the outer leaves. Continue trimming the sprouts until all large leaves are removed. Reserve any leftover sprouts for another use (such as roasting or shredding for a salad).

Place sprout leaves in a bowl and toss with olive oil, vinegar, and salt. Transfer to the baking sheet in a single, even layer.

Roast for 7 to 10 minutes until crisp and slightly browned. Remove from oven and let cool completely on baking sheet before serving or storing.

Scan here to shop the recipe

What can't cauliflower do? In this recipe from keto meal prep maestro **Bobby Parrish**, aka *@flavcity*, it takes the place of potatoes—proving you can still enjoy a creamy, hearty mash while avoiding starchy foods. Garlic, butter, and cheese keep it rich and flavorful.

SNACKS & SIDES

Cauliflower Mash

Gluten-Free   Grain-Free   Egg-Free

INGREDIENTS

1 tablespoon plus 1/4 teaspoon salt, divided, plus more to taste

1 large head of cauliflower, cut into bite-sized florets

4 garlic cloves, peeled

1/4 cup grated Parmesan or Pecorino Romano cheese

1 tablespoon Thrive Market Organic Ghee

Thrive Market Organic Whole Black Peppercorns, freshly ground

INSTRUCTIONS

Bring a large pot of water to a boil and add 1 tablespoon of salt. Add cauliflower florets and garlic; boil until cauliflower is just soft enough to mash with a fork, about 7 to 10 minutes. (Avoid overcooking or the mash will be too loose).

Drain the cauliflower and garlic, reserving 1 cup of water. Transfer cauliflower to a blender along with cheese, ghee, 1/4 teaspoon of salt, and a few cracks of pepper.

Blend until smooth and creamy, using a plunging stick (if your blender has 1) to help blend all of the cauliflower. Add reserved water 1 tablespoon at a time if the mash is too thick. Season to taste with additional salt and pepper if desired.

Scan here to shop the recipe

Our Organic Medjool Dates come from California's Coachella Valley, where they get natural sweetness from the desert sun.

Dessert

Grills aren't just for burgers and steaks—this dessert recipe will broaden your grilling repertoire. Naturally sweet peaches caramelize when they hit the heat, becoming soft and warm—like pie filling with a hint of smokiness. Topped with cool, creamy yogurt and a handful of granola, they become the ideal summer dessert: simple, seasonal, delicious.

DESSERT

Grilled Peaches With Yogurt & Granola

Gluten-Free   Grain-Free   Egg-Free

INGREDIENTS

1 1/2 cups plain Greek yogurt (or dairy-free yogurt of your choice)

1 teaspoon Thrive Market Organic Vanilla Extract

4 ripe peaches

2 to 3 tablespoons melted Thrive Market Organic Virgin Coconut Oil

Granola of choice, to serve (try Thrive Market Organic Grain-Free Vanilla Cinna-Yum Granola or Homemade Coconut Granola, page 32)

Thrive Market Organic Honey, to serve

INSTRUCTIONS

In a small bowl, combine yogurt and vanilla extract. Set aside.

Halve peaches, remove pits, and brush cut sides with coconut oil. Heat a grill pan or grill to medium. Place peaches cut side down on the grill and cook until grill marks appear and peaches are tender, 4 to 6 minutes.

Top peaches with a dollop of vanilla-yogurt mixture, a sprinkle of granola, and a drizzle of honey to serve.

Scan here to shop the recipe

Created by **Megan Mitchell**, this fudgy treat is full of rich chocolate flavor, short on prep time, and enough for two hearty servings, making it the ideal date-night dessert (just add two spoons—and a scoop of plant-based vanilla ice cream, if you wish).

DESSERT

Vegan Olive Oil Skillet Brownies

Gluten-Free   Dairy-Free   Vegan   Egg-Free

INGREDIENTS

1/2 cup Thrive Market Organic Dark Chocolate Chips, plus more for sprinkling

1/4 cup Thrive Market Organic Extra Virgin Olive Oil, plus more for coating pan

1/4 cup Thrive Market Organic Maple Syrup

1/2 teaspoon Thrive Market Organic Vanilla Extract

1/2 cup gluten-free flour

2 tablespoons cocoa powder

1 teaspoon Thrive Market Baking Soda

1/2 teaspoon espresso powder

Pinch of fine sea salt

Flaked sea salt

INSTRUCTIONS

Preheat oven to 325°F. Lightly oil a 7-inch cast-iron skillet, 2 5-ounce ramekins, or any small ovenproof dish. Melt chocolate in a small saucepan over medium-low heat. Whisk until smooth and fully melted, about 2 minutes. Pour into a medium bowl; whisk in olive oil, maple syrup and vanilla.

In a small bowl, whisk flour, cocoa powder, baking soda, espresso powder, and sea salt. Pour dry ingredients on top of chocolate mixture. Combine with a whisk, then finish stirring with a silicone spatula until you no longer see any flour.

Pour into the prepared skillet or dish(es) and sprinkle with a handful of chocolate chips and a large pinch of flaked sea salt. Bake for 15 to 20 minutes, or until set around the edges, puffed up, and with only a slight jiggle in the center.

Let cool for 5 minutes before serving.

Scan here to shop the recipe

With only four main ingredients, the simplicity of this recipe—from **Katie Wells** of **Wellness Mama** makes it a quick fix for last-minute cravings. Depending on your diet, feel free to serve with an extra flourish of whipped cream or ice cream.

DESSERT

Very Berry Cobbler

Gluten-Free   Grain-Free   Dairy-Free   Vegan   Egg-Free

INGREDIENTS

4 cups strawberries, blackberries, blueberries, raspberries, or an assorted mix (fresh or frozen)

1 cup Thrive Market Almond Flour

1/4 cup Thrive Market Organic Virgin Coconut Oil or butter

1 teaspoon Thrive Market Organic Vanilla Extract

Thrive Market Organic Stevia, Organic Honey, or Organic Maple Syrup, to taste (optional)

INSTRUCTIONS

Preheat oven to 375°F and grease an 8x8 inch baking dish with coconut oil or butter. Place berries in the baking dish.

Combine almond flour, coconut oil or butter, and vanilla with your hands until it forms a crumbly consistency. You may need to adjust the almond flour up or down slightly. If you're using stevia, you can add a small amount to the topping at this point.

Crumble the topping over the berries. Place the baking dish in the oven and bake until topping is lightly golden brown (about 20 minutes if you used fresh berries, or 30 to 40 minutes if you used frozen).

Once cobbler is finished, allow to cool slightly before serving, drizzled with honey or maple syrup as desired.

Scan here to shop the recipe

The classic combination of peanut butter and jelly gets a playful upgrade in these snack-sized cookie sandwiches. Assembling the stacks is a fun activity for little ones, and the irresistible mix of dark chocolate, smooth almond butter, tart raspberry, and crunchy cracker is a treat for kids of all ages.

DESSERT

Chocolate, Almond Butter & Jam Cracker Sandwiches

Gluten-Free   Grain-Free   Dairy-Free   Vegan   Egg-Free

INGREDIENTS

40 gluten-free crackers

1/2 cup Thrive Market Organic Almond Butter

1/3 cup Thrive Market Organic Raspberry Fruit Spread

10 ounces Organic Dark Chocolate Chips

INSTRUCTIONS

Spread almond butter on 1 side of 20 crackers. Spread jam on 1 side of the other 20 crackers. Sandwich crackers together. Place on a cooling rack set on top of a baking sheet.

Melt the chocolate in a heat-proof bowl placed over a pot of simmering water, whisking. Once fully melted and smooth, remove from heat and let cool slightly.

Spoon melted chocolate over cracker sandwiches. Let chocolate set before serving, refrigerating if necessary.

Scan here to shop the recipe

This recipe nails the sweet-and-salty balance—and with just four ingredients, it couldn't be easier to make. Wow your dinner guests (or keep the whole batch for yourself).

DESSERT

Sea Salt Caramel Brittle

Gluten-Free   Grain-Free   Egg-Free

INGREDIENTS

1 (4-ounce) box almond flour crackers

2 sticks unsalted butter

1 cup Thrive Market Organic Maple Syrup

1 teaspoon flaky sea salt

INSTRUCTIONS

Line a baking sheet with a silicone mat and arrange crackers on the tray in a single layer.

Melt butter and maple syrup in a saucepan over medium-high heat. Simmer for 10 to 20 minutes, stirring frequently to keep the liquid from boiling over. The mixture should be a dark amber color and the consistency of caramel.

Quickly pour the caramel mixture over the crackers and spread with a spatula, if necessary. Sprinkle with flaky sea salt.

Let cool until the caramel hardens, then break into large pieces before serving.

Scan here to shop the recipe

Limiting carbs? With almond flour and your choice of alternative sweetener, this recipe—from keto diet experts **Thomas and Amber DeLauer**—will bring a smile to your face.

DESSERT

Keto Pumpkin Spice Donuts

Gluten-Free   Grain-Free

INGREDIENTS

For the Donuts

4 eggs, beaten

5 tablespoons softened Thrive Market Organic Coconut Cream (or heavy cream)

5 tablespoons water

1/2 cup grass-fed melted butter (or Thrive Market Organic Virgin Coconut Oil & a pinch of salt)

2 tablespoons softened cream cheese (or substitute dairy-free cream cheese)

2 teaspoons Thrive Market Organic Vanilla Extract

2 1/4 cups Thrive Market Almond Flour

1 1/4 teaspoons Thrive Market Baking Powder

1/2 teaspoon Thrive Market Baking Soda

2 tablespoons pumpkin pie spice, or more to taste

1 cup Thrive Market Organic Stevia (or your preferred keto-friendly sweetener)

Thrive Market Organic Virgin Coconut Oil, for brushing the pan

For the Icing

6 ounces cream cheese

1/8 cup Thrive Market Organic Stevia

2 teaspoons Thrive Market Organic Vanilla Extract

1–2 teaspoons Thrive Market Organic Ground Cinnamon

1/4 cup sliced almonds (optional, for garnish)

INSTRUCTIONS

Preheat oven to 350°F.

Beat eggs and cream in a stand mixer or with a hand mixer. While still mixing, add the water, butter, cream cheese, and vanilla.

Next, add the almond flour, baking powder, baking soda, spice, and stevia and mix until smooth. If the batter seems too thin, you can add an extra tablespoon of almond flour. If it seems too thick, add an extra tablespoon of water. It should be thick enough to scoop easily with a spoon.

Brush donut molds with coconut oil. Divide the batter evenly amongst the donut molds.

Bake for 15 to 18 minutes, or until the edges are slightly brown, the tops are firm, and a toothpick inserted into the donut comes out clean. Remove from molds and allow to cool on a wire rack.

While donuts are cooling, make the frosting by whisking together the softened cream cheese, stevia, and vanilla. Spread the frosting onto the donuts and sprinkle with cinnamon and the sliced almonds, if using.

Scan here to shop the recipe

The magic ingredient in chef **Megan Mitchell**'s grown-up shake—aside from bourbon, of course—is broiler-charred marshmallows. With their sweetness offset by a slightly smoky flavor, they'll bring the cozy campfire vibes.

DESSERT

Boozy Toasted Marshmallow Milkshake

Gluten-Free   Grain-Free   Dairy-Free   Vegan   Egg-Free

INGREDIENTS

Thrive Market Organic
Coconut Oil Spray

1/2 (10-ounce) bag vegan
marshmallows (about 12 or 13
marshmallows)

1/2 cup Thrive Market Organic
Coconut Milk, Regular

1/4 cup bourbon

1 vanilla bean pod,
seeds scraped out

1 tablespoon Thrive Market
Organic Vanilla Extract

1 pint vegan coconut ice cream

Coconut whipped cream, for garnish

INSTRUCTIONS

Preheat broiler. Line a baking sheet with foil and lightly mist with coconut oil spray. Arrange marshmallows, leaving space around each 1. Broil 2 to 3 minutes, or until charred. Let cool.

Add charred marshmallows to a high-speed blender, along with coconut milk, bourbon, vanilla bean seeds, and vanilla extract; blend until a thick, caramel-colored sauce forms. Add ice cream and blend until smooth. Pour into 2 or 3 short glasses. Top with coconut whipped cream, if using.

If you have leftover marshmallows, you can place them on a long metal skewer and quickly char them over an open flame. Add 1 to 2 per glass, if desired.

*Scan here to
shop the recipe*

If you thought gummy vitamins were genius, wait until you try these chocolate morsels, made with collagen peptides for a protein boost. You can keep them in the fridge for up to a week, but with their divine chocolate flavor and melt-in-your-mouth texture, it's doubtful they'll last that long.

DESSERT

Keto Collagen Brownie Bombs

Gluten-Free   Grain-Free   Egg-Free

INGREDIENTS

4 ounces cream cheese, softened

1/4 cup Thrive Market Organic Almond Butter

1/4 cup Thrive Market Organic Cacao Powder, plus more for dusting

2 scoops Thrive Market Grass-Fed Collagen Peptides, Chocolate

3 to 4 tablespoons Thrive Market Switch

2 tablespoons Thrive Market Organic Virgin Coconut Oil, melted

1/3 cup stevia-sweetened mini chocolate chips

INSTRUCTIONS

Add all ingredients except chocolate chips to a food processor and process until smooth. Add chocolate chips and pulse a few times to mix.

Using a tablespoon, scoop mixture into balls and place on a parchment-lined baking sheet; freeze for 10 minutes. Gently roll the balls between the palms of your hands until round. Return to freezer for another 10 minutes. Dust with cacao powder before serving.

Scan here to shop the recipe

Who can resist a chocolate chip cookie fresh from the oven? This version of the classic treat gets a delectably nutty upgrade with hazelnut flour. Big chunks (not chips) of chocolate keep it indulgent enough without refined sugar.

DESSERT

Hazelnut Chocolate Chunk Cookies

Gluten-Free   Grain-Free   Dairy-Free   Vegan   Egg-Free

INGREDIENTS

2 cups Thrive Market Non-GMO Hazelnut Meal/Flour

1 cup Thrive Market Almond Flour

1 teaspoon sea salt

3/4 teaspoon Thrive Market Baking Soda

1/2 cup melted Thrive Market Organic Virgin Coconut Oil

1/2 cup Thrive Market Organic Maple Syrup

1 tablespoon Thrive Market Organic Vanilla Extract

1 1/4 cups chocolate, chopped

INSTRUCTIONS

Preheat oven to 350°F and line a baking sheet with parchment paper.

In a large bowl, whisk together hazelnut flour, almond flour, sea salt, and baking soda.

In a small bowl, whisk together coconut oil, maple syrup, and vanilla. Stir wet ingredients into dry ingredients until combined. Stir in chocolate.

Place 1 1/2-inch balls of batter 1 inch apart on baking sheet and lightly press down on each with your palm. Bake for 8 to 10 minutes. Let cool on baking sheet.

Scan here to shop the recipe

The chewy texture of these coconut macaroons, created by **Danielle Walker** of **Against All Grain**, is made all the more irresistible by the festive combination of dark chocolate and bracing peppermint.

DESSERT

Peppermint Chocolate Macaroons

Gluten-Free   Grain-Free   Dairy-Free

INGREDIENTS

3 cups Thrive Market
Organic Shredded Coconut

1/2 cup Thrive Market
Organic Cacao Powder

1/2 cup Thrive Market
Organic Honey

1/2 cup Thrive Market
Organic Coconut Milk

1/2 teaspoon Thrive Market
Organic Peppermint Extract

1/4 teaspoon Thrive Market
Organic Vanilla Extract

1 egg white

Dash of sea salt

INSTRUCTIONS

Preheat oven to 325°F. Line a cookie sheet with parchment paper.

Combine the coconut, cacao powder, honey, coconut milk, peppermint extract, and vanilla extract in a bowl.

In the bowl of a stand mixer, or using an electric hand mixer, beat the egg white with a small pinch of salt for 1 to 2 minutes until soft peaks form when you lift the mixer out.

Fold the egg white into the coconut mixture and mix gently until fully combined.

Using a cookie scoop or tablespoon, scoop out balls of dough, packing tightly either by lightly knocking the scoop onto the side of the bowl or pushing the dough down with your fingers.

Place the dough balls on the cookie sheet and bake for 30 minutes, rotating the sheet halfway through. Cool on a wire cooling rack.

Optionally, melt dark chocolate with 1/4 teaspoon of peppermint extract, then dip the bottoms of the macaroons in the mixture and allow to set before serving.

Scan here to shop the recipe

Drinks

Your average coffee shop latte gets a nutrient-dense boost with this trio of superfood brews. There's a caffeine-free refresher powered by Moringa (a vitamin- and mineral-rich plant native to India); a glow-boosting vanilla latte with collagen created by **Katie Wells** of **Wellness Mama**; and a turmeric-spiced blend that offers a dose of nourishing protein. Note that whenever you're blending hot liquids, use a blender with an opening in the lid for safety—or try a handheld blender or frother.

Superfood Vanilla Latte

Gluten-Free

Grain-Free

Egg-Free

YIELD 1 SERVING
TOTAL TIME 5 MINUTES

INGREDIENTS

1 cup brewed coffee or herbal coffee alternative (for best results, brew coffee in a French press)

1 tablespoon grass-fed butter or Thrive Market Organic Ghee

1 tablespoon Thrive Market Organic Virgin Coconut Oil or Organic MCT Oil

1 tablespoon Thrive Market Grass-Fed Collagen Peptides

1/2 teaspoon Thrive Market Organic Vanilla Extract

INSTRUCTIONS

Place brewed coffee, butter, coconut oil/MCT oil, collagen peptides, and vanilla in a blender. Blend on high for 10 to 15 seconds until frothy.

Vegan Lemon Moringa Latte

Gluten-Free   Grain-Free   Dairy-Free   Vegan   Egg-Free

YIELD 1 SERVING
TOTAL TIME 7 MINUTES

INGREDIENTS

1/2 cup water

1 bag rooibos tea

3/4 cup Thrive Market Organic Coconut Milk, hot

1 scoop Moringa leaf powder

1 tablespoon Thrive Market Organic Maple Syrup

1 tablespoon fresh lemon juice

INSTRUCTIONS

Bring water to a boil in a small saucepan over medium heat. Pour into a mug and steep tea bag for 5 minutes; discard tea bag. While tea steeps, add hot coconut milk, Moringa powder, maple syrup, and lemon juice to a blender; process until combined. Pour into the tea mug, stir, and serve.

Golden Milk Latte

Gluten-Free   Grain-Free   Dairy-Free   Egg-Free

YIELD 1 SERVING
TOTAL TIME 10 MINUTES

INGREDIENTS

1 1/2 cups Thrive Market Organic Almond Beverage

1 tablespoon Thrive Market Organic Honey

1/2 teaspoon Thrive Market Organic Turmeric Powder

1/4 teaspoon Thrive Market Organic Ground Ginger

Pinch Thrive Market Organic Ground Pepper

1/2 scoop Organic Bone Broth Protein Turmeric

Thrive Market Organic Ground Cinnamon, for garnish

INSTRUCTIONS

Whisk together almond milk, honey, turmeric, ginger, and pepper in a small saucepan over low heat for 5 minutes.

Pour into a blender and add protein powder; blend until frothy, about 1 minute. Pour latte into a mug and sprinkle with cinnamon.

Megan Mitchell plays bartender for this roundup of effortlessly festive cocktails made with sparkling wine: an elegant, berry-hued concoction with immunity benefits; a sophisticated play on a mimosa with grapefruit and fresh herbs; and a frothy mix of citrus and mint. Now all you need is a reason to celebrate.

Gluten-Free Grain-Free Dairy-Free Vegan Egg-Free Nut-Free

Grapefruit & Sage Sparkling Cocktail

YIELD 2 COCKTAILS
TOTAL TIME 10 MINUTES

INGREDIENTS

Sparkling wine

2 ruby red grapefruits, halved

Grapefruit bitters

Fresh sage leaves

INSTRUCTIONS

First, make the grapefruit juice: Warm a medium-sized nonstick skillet over medium heat. Place grapefruit slices cut side down into the hot pan and sear 2 to 3 minutes, or until charred. Once cool enough to handle, squeeze through a fine mesh strainer into a clean bowl. (You'll need 1/2 cup of juice for each cocktail.)

To make the cocktails, pour 1/2 cup charred grapefruit juice into each champagne coupe. Top with sparkling wine and a few dashes of bitters. Garnish with sage leaves.

Elderberry Fizz

Gluten-Free Grain-Free Dairy-Free Vegan Egg-Free Nut-Free

YIELD 2 COCKTAILS
TOTAL TIME 5 MINUTES

INGREDIENTS

Sparkling wine

2 teaspoons St. Germain

2 teaspoons wellmade by Thrive Market Organic Elderberry Syrup

2 thyme sprigs

INSTRUCTIONS

Fill champagne coupes 3/4-full with sparkling wine. Add St. Germain and elderberry syrup; stir. Top each drink with a thyme sprig and serve.

Blood Orange Spritz

Gluten-Free   Grain-Free   Dairy-Free   Nut-Free

YIELD 2 COCKTAILS
TOTAL TIME 10 MINUTES

INGREDIENTS

Ice

2 blood oranges, juiced
(about 1/2 cup of juice)

1 small lemon, juiced

1 egg white

1/4 cup vodka

Sparkling wine

Fresh mint leaves

INSTRUCTIONS

Fill a cocktail shaker halfway with ice. Add blood orange juice, lemon juice, egg white, and vodka; vigorously shake for 1 minute. Strain into 2 champagne coupes; top with sparkling wine and garnish with mint leaves.

Wake up to a new ritual, compliments of Moon Juice Founder **Amanda Chantal Bacon**, who says she's been making this tonic for years to reap its creativity-boosting, focus-enhancing benefits. A combination of Moon Juice's cult-status superfood blends gives this drink its magic.

Moon Juice Morning Tonic

Gluten-Free Grain-Free Dairy-Free Vegan Egg-Free Nut-Free

YIELD 1 SERVING
TOTAL TIME 5 MINUTES

INGREDIENTS

1 cup water or milk of choice (try Thrive Market Organic Almond or Oat Beverage), warm

2 tablespoons Moon Juice Vegan Collagen Protect®

1 teaspoon Thrive Market Organic Instant Coffee

1 teaspoon Moon Juice Sex Dust®

1 teaspoon Moon Juice Brain Dust®

INSTRUCTIONS

Combine all ingredients in a blender (make sure to use one with a hole in the lid for safety; you can also use a handheld blender or frother). Blend on high until fully combined and frothy.

A zingy mix of fresh citrus and warming spices, **Megan Mitchell**'s wellness shot can be sipped on its own for a plant-powered immunity boost, or used as the base ingredient in the trio of fresh cocktails on the next page.

Wellness Shot

Gluten-Free Grain-Free Dairy-Free Vegan Egg-Free Nut-Free

YIELD 1 1/2 TO 2 CUPS
TOTAL TIME 10 MINUTES

INGREDIENTS

4 lemons, juiced

3 navel oranges, juiced

2 ruby red grapefruits, juiced

1 3-inch piece ginger, peeled and finely grated

1 tablespoon Thrive Market Organic Turmeric Powder

1 teaspoon Thrive Market Organic Cayenne Pepper

INSTRUCTIONS

Combine all ingredients in a small pitcher or liquid measuring cup; whisk. Drink 1/4 to 1/2 cup daily, or as needed. Refrigerate, covered, up to 1 week.

n Mitchell's trio of cocktails with benefits—a refreshing blend of tequila and elderflower, a bitter but balanced sparkler, and a superfood spin on a whiskey sour—all start with her spicy and vibrant Wellness Shot (page 163).

Triple Citrus Whiskey Cocktail

Gluten-Free Grain-Free Dairy-Free Nut-Free

YIELD 1 COCKTAIL
TOTAL TIME 5 MINUTES

INGREDIENTS

1/4 cup Wellness Shot

1/4 cup whiskey

1 tablespoon Thrive Market Organic Honey

1 egg white

1 large ice cube

Sprig of fresh rosemary

INSTRUCTIONS

Combine the Wellness Shot, whiskey, honey, and egg white in a cocktail shaker or 16-ounce mason jar. Fill halfway with ice, close tightly, and shake vigorously for 1 minute until the egg white is foamy.

Place a large ice cube in a rocks glass. Using a small, fine mesh strainer, pour the drink into the glass and garnish with a rosemary sprig. Serve.

Superfood Sunrise

Gluten-Free Grain-Free Dairy-Free Vegan Egg-Free Nut-Free

YIELD 1 COCKTAIL
TOTAL TIME 5 MINUTES

INGREDIENTS

1/2 cup Wellness Shot

1/4 cup tequila blanco

1 tablespoon Thrive Market Organic Maple Syrup

1 tablespoon St. Germain

Kosher salt

INSTRUCTIONS

Combine all ingredients in a cocktail shaker or 16-ounce mason jar. Fill with ice, close tightly, and shake for 30 to 45 seconds.

Using a citrus rind left over from making the Wellness Shot, wet the rim of a rocks glass, and then press glass into a small dish filled with kosher salt. Pour cocktail into the glass, adding more ice if needed. Serve.

Crimson Spritz

Gluten-Free Grain-Free Dairy-Free Vegan Egg-Free Nut-Free

YIELD 1 COCKTAIL
TOTAL TIME 5 MINUTES

INGREDIENTS

1/2 cup Wellness Shot

1/4 cup vodka

1 tablespoon Thrive Market Organic Maple Syrup

Seltzer or club soda

Aperol

INSTRUCTIONS

Combine the Wellness Shot, vodka, and maple syrup in a cocktail shaker or 16-ounce mason jar. Fill with ice, close tightly, and shake for 30 to 45 seconds.

Pour cocktail into a highball glass. Top with soda water and a splash of Aperol. Serve.

Index

ACKNOWLEDGEMENTS

CONTENT DIRECTION
Amy Wicks
Kirby Stirland

CREATIVE DIRECTION
Elise Crevier

PHOTOGRAPHY
Teri Lyn Fisher
Matthew Schulert
Elisha Knight
Marylene Mey
Melissa Castro

FOOD STYLING
Marian Cairns
Megan Hubbell
Natalie Drobny

PRODUCTION
Marlie Crisafulli

ART DIRECTION & DESIGN
Brains on Fire
Gustavo Delgado
Benjamin Hart
Sean Madden
Sara Nicely
Amy Taylor

Additionally, we couldn't have done this without:
Alicia Angulo
Jason Bidart
Cassandra Bodzak
Yasmine Borno
Lauren Bondell
Schuyler Blyth
Christina Chin
Carolyn Clark
Lily Comba
Julianna Crozier
Kristin DeSimone
Jenna Engleman
Angela Gaines
Nick Green
Nicole Gulotta
Mike Hacaga
Sylvia Hartley
Ian Hladun
Wade Johnson
Shira Karsen
Noel Larson
Tiffany Lee
Laura Levin
Kerrie Lopez
Kendall Lowery
Jeremiah McElwee
Nicole McMillen
Christine McNerney
Courtney Merfeld
Erin Mosbaugh
Merce Muse
Josh Nadel
Jessica Nguyen
Rachel Parent
Katie Parker
Amina Pasha
Michelle Pellizzon
Kendall Sargeant
Sasha Siddhartha
Arianna Stern
Carole Weber
Jenn Welsch

Certified
B
Corporation

©Copyright 2021 Thrive Market, Inc. All rights reserved. Thrive Market, the Thrive Market logo and Belong to a Better Market are registered trademarks, and Healthy Living Made Easy is a trademark of Thrive Market. Inc. All other trademarks property of their respective owners. Printed in Canada.